BEYOND THE TRUST GAP

FORGING A NEW PARTNERSHIP BETWEEN MANAGERS AND THEIR EMPLOYERS

Thomas R. Horton
Peter C. Reid

BUSINESS ONE IRWIN
Homewood, Illinois 60430

Executive editor: Jeffrey Krames
Project editor: Karen J. Murphy
Production manager: Diane Palmer
Compositor: BookMasters, Inc.
Typeface: 11/13 Century Schoolbook
Printer: The Book Press, Inc.

Library of Congress Cataloging-in-Publication Data
Horton, Thomas R.
    Beyond the trust gap : forging a new partnership between managers
and their employers / Thomas R. Horton, Peter C. Reid.
        p.   cm.
    Includes index.
    ISBN 1-55623-269-1
        1. Executives—United States—Interviews. 2. Employee morale.
3. Leadership. 4. Trust (Psychology) I. Reid, Peter C.
II. Title.
HD38.25.U6H66   1991
658.4'092—dc20   90-42474
                                                                CIP

Printed in the United States of America
1 2 3 4 5 6 7 8 9 0 BP 7 6 5 4 3 2 1 0

To Marilou Horton and Carol Reid who,
although perhaps sorely tempted,
did not outplace us during the course of this project.

PREFACE

As we were writing this book, one thing amazed us. Among most corporate leaders there seemed to be very little sense of urgency about addressing what we believe is one of the overriding crises facing U.S. business today: the ruptured relations between managers and their employers. If one were to sum up the attitudes of many top executives, it would run something like this: "Sure, there's been some bloodletting, and some people have been hurt. Maybe morale is a little down right now. But not to worry—things will be back to normal soon. After all, our managers are getting paid, aren't they?"

Corporate leaders with this attitude are totally missing the point—just as they missed the point 20 years ago when global competition began nibbling away at their domination of world markets. For that they have paid a heavy price in lost market share and virtual elimination from many burgeoning businesses such as consumer electronics and machine tools.

Now they are failing to understand the seriousness of what has happened to their relationships with their managers. What they see as a temporary blip that will soon be erased by the passage of time is actually a profound change in the way that managers view the corporations for which they are working—a change that threatens to derail U.S. business in its rush for global success.

This change is succinctly and eloquently summed up in the phrase *trust gap*. When *Fortune* magazine used that as a title for an article on employee-management relations in December 1989, the author commented that "employees would like nothing better than to push a butter knife slowly through the boss's well-intentioned heart." No doubt the boss would be surprised by such an assault—it is a rare CEO who bothers to find out what his or her "loyal" underlings really think.

If CEOs <u>were</u> to investigate the attitudes of their managers and other employees, some wouldn't believe what they find, while others would call the employees crybabies. Some would begin to recognize that they are part of the problem and would take positive actions to close the trust gap. A few already have.

But it is rather late in the game to rely on only a handful of enlightened business leaders to repair the damage. The trust gap is wider than ever. It is spreading rapidly through U.S. business as more and more companies go "mean and lean," which almost always entails downsizing through layoffs. Employers have rapidly killed off the old unwritten employment contract that virtually guaranteed job security, promotions, and steady raises. Now this contract must speedily be replaced because, as we head into the 1990s, the vacuum it has left is being filled by mistrust, cynicism, and just plain fear. These are not the qualities of a motivated, productive team of managers.

In writing this book, we asked ourselves: *What can replace the old contract that will help to close the trust gap and forge a new partnership between managers and employers?* First, we examined the covenant that once existed between them and now has been irrevocably broken.

This covenant was perhaps best expressed by Thomas J. Watson, Sr., when he announced IBM's first retirement plan at the company's plant in Endicott, New York, in September

1945. In explaining the program—which was partially financed by his personal income earned during the war—he told IBM employees:

> Worry is just the worst thing that anyone can have. I want to tell you that I consider it my foremost duty in IBM ... to do everything we can do to keep you people from worrying—not only after you retire, but while you are working. Now I do not see any reason why any worthy employee should worry about his job with IBM.

Not everything was good about the old unwritten contract—it was often paternalistic and dictatorial. It could not last forever—nor should it have. But it fostered the kind of employee dedication and commitment that do not exist in most companies today, for two reasons: the way in which the old contract was destroyed and the failure to replace it with a new one of equal value.

How *was* the old contract destroyed? Through in-depth interviews, we explored the devastating impact of downsizings, mergers, takeovers, and leveraged buyouts (LBOs)—not only on those who lost their jobs through these restructurings but also on those who remained to shoulder even more responsibilities after their colleagues were gone. We examined the equally damaging effects of mindless downsizing on the performance of the organization—the costly results of poor planning, inadequate communication, indiscriminate work force cuts, and insensitivity to both the displaced managers and the survivors.

Then we asked ourselves whether downsizing could be done better. We found some positive examples: companies that took the human factor into account rather than focusing solely on the quick bottom-line benefits of dumping thousands of employees.

Finally, we asked both top executives and lower-level managers what could be done by *both* groups to create a more fruitful working relationship between them. The answers we got did not reveal any startling new magic formulas. Instead, they pinpointed some basic principles of organizational leadership that have long been known, but seldom practiced. What *is* new is that U.S. corporate chieftains can no longer afford to ignore these principles. The global economy has generated a whole different ball game— and the teams competing with the United States are fielding more productive, more dedicated players. U.S. business leaders must find a way to work the human equation into their endless number-crunching, or they will have an alienated, disenchanted work force that will never make management's projections come true.

What is also new is that we are heading into a decade of momentous changes in our working population. Business leaders must learn to deal with a shortage of managerial talent, the increasing diversity of the U.S. work force, and the mounting reluctance of many managers to sacrifice their families and personal lives to the demands of stressful, all-consuming jobs.

U.S. managers must also cope with rapidly changing job roles during the 1990s. They must become more self-sufficient as the cradle-to-grave security of the past is replaced by the uncertainty of constant organizational change. And they must be prepared to seek other rewards than the traditional promotions and raises which often came effortlessly in the past.

What evolved from our research and questioning was the model of a new contract between managers and their employers. It retains only vestiges of the old contract, which has been rendered inoperable by the tumultuous forces that are transforming the business world. But we believe that it provides a viable basis for establishing the harmonious, productive relationship that will be so absolutely essential if U.S. business is once more to become a forceful, thriving leader in the world economy.

To bring this new contract to life will not be easy for either managers or their employers. No quick fixes will do the job. But we hope this book will provide both inspiration and practical guidance for those managers and executives at all levels who are willing to embark on a vital mission: bringing trust and teamwork back to the corporate world.

ACKNOWLEDGMENTS

In doing this book, we interviewed more than 100 managers and executives. Although many are named in the text, others preferred anonymity, and there were some whose contributions we lacked space to include. However, we are grateful to all of them for taking time from their busy schedules to talk to us at length about the issues involved in the book.

Our special thanks go to Jim Childs, whose unflagging enthusiasm and helpful suggestions were invaluable.

From Patricia C. Haskell, we received generous helpings of inspiration and sound advice.

Finally, we want to thank the many staff members of the American Management Association who contributed their assistance.

CONTENTS

CHAPTER 1

GOODBYE TO ALL THAT: DISSOLVING THE UNWRITTEN CONTRACT

My first seven years with the company were so great I thought I'd died and gone to heaven. We had a family atmosphere, the training was excellent, and I really felt we were all pulling together to achieve our goals. I looked forward to a career where I could grow as a professional and where my work was recognized and appreciated. Then management made some dumb acquisitions that any kid in the mailroom could have told them wouldn't work. They went from having over a billion dollars in cash to having a billion in debt. To cut costs, they had to restructure and downsize. Morale dropped to zero. I survived three bloodbaths but after each one I had more and more work. Eventually I was doing three people's jobs. When it came my turn to go, I wasn't surprised—I was the right age and was earning enough money to make me a target along with a lot of my friends. Now, when I see friends who are still at the company and ask them how they're doing, they say, "What the hell, they've capped my salary; I've no room for advancement; and they don't listen to me. So I'm just sitting there and keeping a low profile and doing my job and not offering anything."

—A former middle manager for a large cosmetics firm— now a consultant

No more guarantees of lifetime employment. No more automatic salary increases. No more promotions for just showing up. No more bankable career ladders. The unwritten contract between employers and their middle managers that promised all those things is dead and buried. But there's no time for mourning. We must look ahead and ask: What should succeed the old contract? Can we restore the bonds of trust on realistic grounds? And if so, how?

Answers are hard to come by—some would say impossible. But we must try, because finding the answers is a vital part of the answer to an even bigger issue: whether the United States will become a second-rate economic force in the 1990s. Neglect of the eroding relationships between managers and their employers will leave the United States ill-equipped to compete successfully in a global market.

U.S. corporations cannot restore the old contract—it no longer meets the needs of a kaleidoscopic business world. And some elements of the old contract worked against a mature relationship between an employer and its managers. It did give employees a feeling of security and stimulated a sense of loyalty. At the same time, it made them almost totally dependent, incapable of fending for themselves. It was primarily a parental relationship.

But the contract was based on certain values that seem to have been forgotten today. There was a caring concern for employees as individuals, a belief that employers had a commitment to their people. Even though the old contract is history, we can restore these lost values—and apply them to building a more mature relationship between the organization and the manager, a relationship that sensibly balances the needs of both and recognizes the realities of a new business age. This book is aimed at helping organizations and managers alike to achieve that goal.

THE OLD CONTRACT: "WE'LL TAKE CARE OF YOU"

Of course, new employees were not handed signed guarantees of lifetime job security. But they were often given *implied* promises by both the employee manual and their bosses. It was assumed that when they signed on with One Big Happy Family, Inc., they were still going to be around to collect their gold service pins 25 years later. Job-hopping was not in vogue. One production manager told us:

> I worked for a large, worldwide corporation with a feeling of rock-solid permanence. When I was hired in 1972, I was told that the only way I could lose my job was through fighting, theft, or lewd behavior. I had the feeling that I could retire there if I wanted to.

Another manager, in a service company, reported that when he was hired in 1968 he was promised lifetime employment so long as he didn't steal company funds. A returning World War II veteran who applied at IBM shortly after the war was advised to consult his wife before accepting a job because once you came aboard you were a member of the corporate family for life.

So there was an *unwritten* contract between the organization and the manager. If a manager were to put it into words it would probably sound something like this:

> To ensure the present and future prosperity of the company, I will work energetically, loyally, single-mindedly at getting things done through other people and do whatever the company needs to have done no matter how much time it takes and even if the job is unpleasant.
> In return, I will receive job security, fair compensation (some of which will be applied to future retirement benefits), steady upward promotions when deserved, and appropriate recognition of my individual contribution.

For many years after World War II, most managers took this contract for granted—it was a given. They were caught up in the excitement of an expanding U.S. economy and their own expanding job responsibilities. New technologies were exploding. America was becoming the world's leading economic power. U.S. living standards were shooting upward. There seemed to be no limit to growth.

Promotions came readily and frequently, to both outstanding performers and those who were only adequate. For many managers, their jobs had great meaning and, indeed, virtually defined them. For such fulfilled and highly committed managers, there was no need to worry about that unwritten "contract." Indeed, there seemed to be no need for such an agreement. After all, they were virtually indispensable to their employers—or so they thought. Without their contributions, the seemingly endless expansion of the U.S. economy would grind to a halt. This was the age of William Whyte's *Organization Man*. As he wrote in his 1956 classic:

> They are the ones of our middle class who have left home, spiritually as well as physically, to take the vows of organization life, and it is they who are the mind and soul of our great self-perpetuating institutions.

Perhaps it was all too easy to rack up corporate profits. With the insatiable consumer demand of the postwar years, there was no such thing as a mature market. U.S. consumers couldn't get enough toasters, washing machines, cars, and television sets—all made in America. As these markets constantly grew, so did the companies that supplied them. U.S. organization charts sprouted new branches, limbs, shoots, suckers, and thick underbrush. In those corporate thickets resided not only committed managers and workaholics but a growing number of unfulfilled and disillusioned middle managers whose jobs held no meaning and little reward beyond that provided by the unwritten contract. After all, during this era of unbridled growth and virtually guaranteed lifetime employment, there had to be some place to put employees like old Bill, who had conquered a sales territory but had not measured up after being promoted to headquarters. Whole new kinds of support groups proliferated, and the bushy corporate tree was adorned with such job titles as *assistant to* or *coordinator*. Corporations developed excessive layers of management and became badly infected with bureaucratic bloat. Many jobs were boring, laden with interminable paperwork of dubious significance. Managers became links in an endless chain, message-carriers to higher and lower levels. Their decision-making influence was minimal, and they had to carry out strategies they had no hand in formulating.

But they still had security. Joining a large corporation provided them with a solid foundation on which they could build their lives, knowing that probably even a depression would not land them on the street. William Whyte described their attitudes this way:

> When (college seniors) explained a preference for the big corporation, they did so largely on grounds of security. When I talked to students in 1949, on almost every campus I heard one recurring theme: adventure was all very well, but it was smarter to make a compromise in order to get a depression-proof sanctuary. "I don't think AT&T is very exciting," one senior put it, "but that's the company I'd like to join. If a depression comes there will always be an AT&T." Another favorite was the food industry: "People always have to eat." Corporation recruiters were unsettled to find that seniors seemed primarily interested in such things as pension benefits and retirement programs.

There was only one way to go in the organization, and that was up (not out or sideways). And in exchange for this security, managers were quite willing to give the company their undying loyalty. As *Training* editor Jack Gordon put it: "Used to be, they'd go to the wall for the company. If you told them to move to Timbuktu, why, they'd pack up and move to Timbuktu. They stuck with a company through thick and thin." (But, as Gordon points out, nobody ever agreed to move to Timbuktu knowing that the Timbuktu branch could be restructured out of existence at any moment and that employees would be stranded there with nothing but some pamphlets explaining how to write a resume.)

"SORRY, YOUR JOB HAS JUST BEEN ELIMINATED"

When the 1980s arrived, the rules of the game changed—violently. Inexorable forces shook the U.S. business world to its roots, and suddenly middle managers became an

For Sale: One Silver Lining, Slightly Tarnished

The corporation had just completed a substantial downsizing in which 10 percent of its middle management employees had retired early or been laid off. One of the surviving managers tried to console a laid-off colleague who had obviously been hard hit by his dismissal.

"Look," she said, "I'm not so sure this is such a great place to work anyway. The pay isn't all that good, promotions are strictly political, and management never listens to us."

"Okay," replied the downsizing victim, "I know all that and I was willing to put up with it. Because there was one thing we always had: security."

endangered species. Thousands were laid off or enticed into early retirement. The unwritten contract was declared null and void, as silently as it had come into existence. The previous widely understood contract appeared not only to have been unwritten, but to have been unwritten in invisible ink.

It's estimated that more than a million middle managers and staff professionals have lost their jobs since 1980—perhaps a third of the total. And the decimation is continuing unabated. Surveys by Right Associates, a Philadelphia-based outplacement firm that ranks second largest in the United States, show that:

- The number of laid-off middle managers—those earning from $40,000 to $60,000—increased 18 percent between 1985 and 1986.
- Between 1986 and 1988, the number of middle-management separations was up 34 percent over the 1985–1986 figure.

The Wall Street Journal estimated that in 1985 alone, 600,000 middle managers landed on the street because of cost cutting, mergers, and takeovers.

In his 1989 survey of downsizing activity among 1,084 companies, American Management Association's Eric Greenberg found that 39.1 percent had cut staff over the 12-month period ending June 1989. The survey covered a cross section of U.S. business: large, midsize, and small companies, including manufacturers and service providers. The average percentage of the work force discharged was 10.1 percent, but a tenth of the companies discharged more than 20 percent of their work forces. Among the reasons given for the downsizings, 43 percent cited a business downturn, actual or expected, 30 percent said "improved staff utilization," 11 percent specified a merger or acquisition, 5 percent mentioned "plant or office obsolescence," and an additional 20 percent cited "other rationales."

In the third quarter of 1989 alone, 12 large companies—including Chrysler, RJR Nabisco, Campbell Soup, and Unisys—laid off a total of 16,720 employees, at least half of them at management levels. In late 1989, General Motors—which had already cut its white-collar work force by 40,000 employees since 1986—revealed plans to cut *another* 25,000 by 1994. At the end of the year, two dozen large companies announced layoffs, early-retirement programs, and restructurings. Among them were Eastman Kodak (5,000 jobs to be eliminated), IBM (10,000), McGraw-Hill (1,000), US West (2,000), and Merrill Lynch (3,000). Even for large companies, these are staggering figures.

Not surprisingly, the Labor Department reported that the number of jobless managers, administrators, and executives in December 1989 shot up by 37,000—more than 12 percent above the figure for the previous December.

A striking aspect of these layoffs was that they consistently violated one of the most "sacred" clauses of the old unwritten employment contract: If you performed well on your job, you would not lose it. This is confirmed by a breakdown of data compiled by Right Associates to identify the reasons that their job candidates were terminated. The data revealed a significant trend between 1985 and 1988. In 1985, 435 candidates had lost their jobs because of job performance, a reduction-in-force, or the elimination of their jobs. Of these, 43 percent were let go because of job performance. In 1988, however, the figures showed that only 33 percent had been terminated because of job performance. *Two thirds were out of a job for reasons entirely unrelated to how well they were performing.*

DOWNSIZING BECOMES A WAY OF LIFE

For many managers, being displaced doesn't happen just once or even twice. O.E. "Ed" Unser, a quality assurance manager in New England, recalls:

> In May 1986, I was working as manager of quality assurance at the Barnstead Company in West Roxbury, Massachusetts. My company was purchased by Forstmann, Little and Company of New York and the operation was moved to Iowa. I was out of a job. That November, I was hired as director of quality assurance and productivity by the James River Company in its Hyde Park, Massachusetts, mill. Before taking the job, I asked for and received assurances from the company's headquarters that it would continue operating in Hyde Park. The following September, the mill closed down permanently. Eight months later I was hired as corporate director of quality assurance at Digital Products, Inc., in Watertown, Massachusetts. Within six months they downsized and I was on the street again. Two months ago I took my present position as quality assurance manager, Fire Control Instruments, Inc., in Newton, Massachusetts. I don't recommend this type of activity to everyone.

It's an uncomfortable truth that in one short decade laying off middle managers has been transformed from a seldom-used desperation measure to an ongoing corporate activity. Downsizing has come out of the closet—it's now re-spectable to "reduce headcount." Not only is it respectable, but it's also often greeted with cheers on Wall Street. The financial community's reasoning is that work force reduc-tions cut into payroll overhead costs and usually generate higher after-tax earnings and stock values. According to one stock analyst at Merrill Lynch, "The nicer a company is to its employees, the less happy Wall Street is." It's no coinci-dence that a company's stock almost always goes up when work force cuts are announced—the few times it doesn't are when Wall Street thinks the cuts weren't deep enough.

Downsizing is now so prevalent in American business that it has spawned a whole new industry: outplacement services. Between 1980 and 1989, the outplacement business grew tenfold, from $35 million to $350 million in revenues—and it is expected to hit $400 million by the end of 1990.

ANGER, FEAR, AND ANXIETY

But what about the major victims of downsizing, middle managers? They're angry. At their employers. At their former employers. At themselves. They feel ill-used, misled, sold out, betrayed. Forget company loyalty. They're now look-ing out for No. 1!

Downsizing *survivors* are often no less resentful and dis-tressed than those who have been cast out. Besides feeling anger over the fate of their former colleagues, they are seething with gripes about unwelcome changes in their own jobs as a result of downsizing:

- They are working harder, with more people to man-age, but their pay increases are slowing down.
- They see their promotional opportunities blocked be-cause there are no jobs to be promoted to.

• Their benefits are being cut back, which in effect shrinks their take-home pay. (The percentage of large U.S. firms paying the full cost of hospital room-and-board charges for employees declined from 53 percent in 1984 to 29 percent in 1988, according to a Hewitt Associates survey.)

Middle managers wonder why they have to take the hit while top management collects mega-bonuses. They ask why their pay is based on performance and that of CEOs is not. And perhaps more than anything else, they feel threatened. If it can happen to their friends, it can happen to them—regardless of the reassurances coming down from the executive suite. The dominant mood in many companies today is fear and anxiety.

The biggest casualty of all is company loyalty—a term that has become almost quaint. In a 1989 Yankelovich Clancy Shulman survey of 520 employed adults, 57 percent said companies were less loyal to their employees than 10 years before—while only 25 percent said companies were more loyal. And 63 percent believed that employees were less loyal to their companies, only 22 percent saying employees were more loyal.

Loyalty has been replaced by mistrust. During our interviews with more than 50 managerial employees, a constant theme was that top management had lost its credibility. Reassurances about layoffs were broken. Top management cut down on middle-management perks in the name of economy, while keeping its own perks intact. The annual report intoned that "People are our most important asset"—while outstanding employee contributions went unrecognized.

A midlevel manager of a medical services company with 400 employees told us:

> My attitude toward my employer suffered in that I no longer believed that my interests were of any concern to the company. When my position was eliminated, I was simply told it

was gone, and I could either accept a demotion or leave. This attitude on the part of the company of indifference to me and my feelings essentially soured my sense of trust and loyalty to the company.

Another survivor is a data processing manager whose electronics company went through two major restructurings within 18 months. He wrote:

> The unwritten contract between middle managers and our corporation has been broken by the corporation with various grades of deception. An important asset of business is gone—trust. Most surviving managers believe that the company is blindly responding to investors' screams that it should build up its cash reserve and its credit rating. Once upon a time, when the unwritten contract was shining with honor, trust, security, competitive wages, and fringe benefits, an equilibrium existed where in return the employer got the employee's dedication, loyalty, and the willingness to provide excellent performance. Now I must find the strength each morning to commute to my office. What was once a "career" is now a "job."

THE FLAME GOES OUT

What's the result for the organization? Middle managers become cautious and risk-averse. They keep their ideas for improving operations to themselves. They do their jobs, but they don't give the extra 10 percent that turns adequate performance into outstanding performance. As one manager told us: "Hey, this is a job and I've got to do it. But I'm not doing it with the flair and enthusiasm of somebody who truly loves it. The thrill is gone."

Sophisticated managers know that the economic world will become more turbulent, not less, and they know they can never expect a return to the job security of the past. Many are ready to accept that—they understand that the world-shaking forces at work are beyond the control of any individual company. What they cannot accept is how their top managements are dealing with these forces. They are convinced that a short-term, bottom-line focus is leading management to make disastrous mistakes—and that they are the ones made to pay for those mistakes. Their confidence in top management's ability is ebbing sharply. Two Opinion Research surveys of middle managers in Fortune 500 companies show a dramatic difference between that confidence in 1983 and in 1988, from 68 percent to 52 percent.

We believe that before there can be any chance of mending the relationships between organizations and their middle managers, top management must recognize the distinction between the impact of outside forces and the impact of their own actions. Corporate leaders cannot remake society all by themselves—they must deal with existing realities. But they can deal with those realities in ways that won't shatter the trust and commitment of their managerial work force. They can act in ways that recognize the worth of their employees and not treat them, as one manager put it, "as if they were as disposable as Kleenex."

Much has been said and written about the "disposability" of middle managers. According to Sir Gordon White, chairman of Hanson Industries, the U.S. subsidiary of the United Kingdom's Hanson, PLC, middle managers only serve to "constipate cash flow." Former GM Chairman Roger Smith called middle managers responsible for the giant company's "frozen bureaucracy." The CEO of a large industrial-equipment company asked us: "Why do we need middle managers any more? We've got computers."

Underlying these extreme statements is a germ of truth. Middle managers today *are* obsolete. However, they are not obsolete because they are middle managers. They are obsolete because they are still doing what middle managers did 20 years ago.

The market for managers is changing rapidly—and managers who don't change their approach to their jobs will not survive long. The managers in demand will be those who can adapt to the new needs of fast-moving, flattened organizations in which one's position in the hierarchy is far less important than one's ability to add value to the organization through innovation and problem solving. Idea entrepreneurs will receive greater rewards than those who simply occupy a box on the organizational chart.

THREE IMPERATIVES FOR MANAGEMENT

In order to inspire and encourage such creativity by its managers, the organization must in turn be creative and innovative in its approaches to managerial development, compensation, and benefits.

Managerial Development. Employers must help their managers to transform themselves from "controllers" to "coaches," to learn from their subordinates rather than knowing it all, to build teams made up of increasingly diverse personnel, to become "leaders" as well as "managers."

Compensation. Employers must learn how to relate appraisal and rewards to what managers know and how they perform rather than how long they've been around. Pay for performance—in all its various forms—must be emphasized over pay for longevity. Compensation that encourages a feeling of "ownership" in the organization is an effective way to bring out that extra 10 percent in managerial effort.

Benefits. As we move into the labor-scarce 1990s, employers will have to compete hard to attract the kind of high-performing managers they need. At the same time, they must take steps to contain the spiraling costs of the quality benefits they must offer. Flexible benefits, low-cost benefits, and employee assistance plans (EAPs) are some of the answers being worked out by innovative organizations.

FORGING A NEW COMPACT

Any effort to repair the ruptured relationship between middle managers and their employers must be based on a "win-win" approach. Right now, most middle managers will tell you they are the losers. What will it take to make them feel like winners again?

There's no simple answer to such a complex challenge. But there is also no reason to say there is no answer at all. Throughout the United States there are large and small companies making serious efforts to cope with the consequences of the broken covenant. From their experiences emerge practical principles that can be applied to any organization willing to tackle the problem in a meaningful way.

But there is one important prerequisite: Both the employer and its middle managers must drop their old ways of thinking. Top management must be open to new attitudes and new approaches. Middle managers must jettison their old expectations and assumptions so that they can renew and reform themselves into productive people controlling their own lives.

Forging a new relationship will not be easy. Not all of today's managers will be adaptable enough to change. Top management may embark on sincere efforts to mend the broken contract but falter under the pressure of short-term, bottom-line demands.

Is it worth the trouble? The answer can only be yes, if one considers the alternative: stressed-out middle managers, diminished commitment, distrust of top management, high turnover of top performers, low morale and productivity.

The solutions we propose are not five-minute fixes or sure-fire formulas. This is long-term problem that demands long-term solutions based on a profound change in the way we look at people and work.

But before solutions can be developed, it is necessary to understand how and why the old contract was broken in the first place.

ON THE ROAD TO SPLITSVILLE

Remember "land yachts"? That was a favorite name for the big, chrome-bedecked cars we used to drive in the 1960s. That was Detroit's Golden Age, when Americans demanded huge, bloated automobiles loaded with nonfunctional ornamental parts. Perhaps not coincidentally, U.S. corporations themselves became land yachts: oversized, cushiony, hard to steer, inefficient, and land-locked. Just as Detroit's cars devoured excessive amounts of fuel, their manufacturers—and most other U.S. companies—required more people and far more money than was necessary to accomplish their tasks.

Then came the oil crisis of the 70s and the invasion of small, fuel-efficient cars from Japan. Both the huge American cars and their makers ran out of gas. For the first time in its life, Detroit had to think small. The era of downsizing had begun in America.

The shrinking of America's automobiles symbolized the end of a postwar binge during which self-indulgent U.S. corporations had become overweight, unwieldy, and complacent. Totally out of shape, they were in no condition to respond rapidly and effectively to the momentous changes taking place in the United States and all over the world: new technology, an information-based society, a faster business tempo, and the onset of global competition. Getting the typical U.S. company to change its ways was about as easy as getting a 100,000-ton oil tanker to reverse course in 10 seconds. Corporations in which it took five layers of management to decide on the color of an office carpet could not be expected to move with agility even when the wave of the future was rushing toward them.

For many U.S. corporate leaders, denying the future seemed easier than responding to it. But along with their heads in the sand something else was buried: the seeds of the ultimate destruction of the old, unspoken employment contract. From these seeds sprouted the crisis of confidence that today is severely hampering U.S. business in its belated efforts to grapple with the forces challenging its preeminence.

"It Can't Happen Here"

There was no shortage of futurists to warn U.S. business leaders that the economic and social scene was turning into a whole new ball game. And there were plenty of warning signals that U.S. dominance over world markets was coming to an end. As David Halberstam points out, Japan had pulled ahead of the United States in the shipbuilding and steel industries by the late 1960s. U.S. consumers showed growing enthusiasm for Japanese consumer products such as cars, cameras, and television sets. But the hubris of U.S. corporations led them to ignore all the danger signs.

Since the close of World War II, they had their markets all to themselves. They were under no pressure to innovate, to increase productivity, to cut costs, to improve quality. If what they had done in the past made them successful, the same approaches would make them successful in the future. They could afford to maintain their overgrown organizational structures and even add to them. As Robert Tomasko pointed out in *Downsizing,* many companies provided abundant management jobs for their employees to move into simply as a carrot to keep them loyal and motivated. In the 1950s and 1960s, the U.S. management work force grew fivefold. By 1980, managers made up 10 percent of the industrial work force—while in Japan the figure was only 4.4. percent. AT&T had more than 100 layers of management on its organization chart. Western Electric Co., its manufacturing arm, had more than 1,000 different managerial titles.

Middle managers themselves often contributed to the complacency that infected U.S. business during the postwar years. Frequently, their primary goal was to be working for a big corporation with a well-known name, rather than to take on the tough challenges of improving productivity and finding better ways of doing things. In selecting a company, many followed the tongue-in-cheek advice of writer Shepherd Mead in his book, *How to Succeed in Business without Really Trying:* "First, it must be *big.* In fact, the bigger the better. It should be big enough so that nobody knows exactly what anyone else is doing. Be sure that yours is a company that *makes* something and that somebody *else* has to make it." During the 1950s and 60s, the corporate womb was warm and cozy, lulling middle managers into a state of relaxation not conducive to continuous innovation and improvement. Many performance appraisals were over-generous, so that even unproductive employees received periodic raises that almost equaled those of higher-performing colleagues. "Don't rock the boat," was the prevailing managerial philosophy.

Global competition blindsided U.S. business because American companies were badly prepared to deal with it. "It can't happen here," business experts told the nation. Said *Business Week* on August 2, 1968: "With over 50 foreign cars already on sale here, the Japanese auto industry isn't likely to carve out a big slice of the U.S. market for itself." (The article overlooked something the Japanese had noticed: The success of the VW Beetle showed that there *was* an American market for small, economical cars.)

The result of this complacency was disastrous for much of U.S. business. In 1969, American manufacturers produced:

- 82 percent of the nation's television sets—now they make almost no television sets at all.
- 88 percent of its cars—in the next 20 years, they lost 30 percent of that market.

• 90 percent of its machine tools—since 1969, they have lost half of the domestic market.

Blaming the "Foreign Devil"

U.S. corporations tended to pin their problems on foreign competition, as if they were guiltless themselves. When all else fails, blame a "foreign devil"—it's a time-honored tactic. But the business upheaval that resulted in tumultuous downsizing and restructuring during the 1980s was caused not so much by the onset of global competition itself as by U.S. inability to meet that competition. If American companies had sufficiently increased their productivity during the previous 20 years, the competitive gap would have been far narrower. But although blue-collar productivity did rise at a steady annual 3 percent during those years, white-collar productivity went down, down, down as corporations became so loaded with superfluous layers of management that they resembled multi-tiered wedding cakes.

Thus, the short-sighted obtuseness of America's business leaders led to the bloodbath of the 1980s, during which a million managers lost their jobs.

Tearing Up the Contract

What finally shattered the old unwritten contract? What brought on the frenzy of downsizing and restructuring that decimated the ranks of middle managers? Many factors played a part:

• Brutal worldwide competition finally made many U.S. corporations realize that they had to move faster—in decision making, product development, production, marketing. But they were hobbled by slow-moving systems and superfluous layers of management.
• The "more, more, more" era ended as markets stopped growing and the only way to thrive was to wrestle market share away from a competitor. U.S. companies

downsized sharply, both to save money and to improve their competitiveness.

- Competition from countries with lower costs invaded and conquered many U.S. markets, forcing U.S. companies to cut their own costs any way they could. Reducing payroll was often the first choice, even though improving systems might have achieved the same goals (in addition to bringing about improved quality).
- Computerization made it possible for the same work to be done by fewer people.
- Computerization also gave nonmanagerial employees direct access to information that formerly had to be provided by their bosses, so fewer bosses were needed.
- The cost of benefits for regular employees shot sky-high, leading companies to rely more on contingent employees, such as contract or temporary employees, who did not get these benefits.
- Mergers created staffing redundancies. If there were three assistant purchasing managers in each of the merging firms, some would have to go.
- Leveraged buyouts generated huge debts that had to be serviced. Often, the required cash flow came from eliminating jobs.
- Pension funds and other institutions became major shareholders, putting pressure on companies for short-term results, higher quarterly earnings, dividends. For many firms, the answer was to reduce payroll costs.
- Feeling the hot breath of corporate raiders on their backs, many companies frantically eliminated jobs to keep their stock prices up.
- Technological change created shorter and shorter product life cycles. This forced companies to make faster decisions and get their new products to the market in less time. To do that required a leaner organization unencumbered by bureaucratic sloth.

The initial response of many U.S. companies to increased global competition also helped to destroy the unwritten contract between employers and their managers. Some companies, of course, made no response at all until it was dangerously late. But others, seeing that their own markets were becoming saturated, responded by diversifying into unrelated businesses where they had no skills and no competitive advantage, Alfred D. Chandler, Isidor Straus Professor Emeritus of Business History at Harvard Business School, points out:

> By the late 1960s, acquisitions and mergers had become almost a mania. The number rose from just over 2,000 in 1965 to over 6,000 in 1969. From 1963 to 1972, close to three fourths of the assets acquired were for product diversification, and one half of these were in unrelated product lines. From 1973 to 1977, one half of all assets acquired through merger and acquisition came from unrelated industries.

The merger and acquisition mania of the 1960s created huge, unwieldy organizations in which top management was increasingly separated from its managers responsible for running the operating divisions. U.S. businesses were even more hobbled in competing with mounting foreign competition than they were before. These managerial weaknesses forced companies to reverse course: They started selling the unrelated businesses they had acquired. Before the mid-1960s, Chandler reports, divestitures were rare. By the early 1970s, they had become commonplace. In 1965 there was only 1 divestiture for every 11 mergers; by 1970 the ratio was 1 to 2.4; and from 1974 to 1977, the ratio was close to or even under 1 to 2.

One result of all these mergers, acquisitions, and divestitures, says Chandler, was to establish the buying and selling of corporations as a business—a very lucrative one.

Thus was the groundwork laid for the next wave of mergers and acquisitions in the 1980s—the Decade of the Deal. But these mergers and acquisitions were fueled by debt rather than equity. The pressure of that debt was one of the major forces that brought on a flood of managerial cutbacks and helped to destroy the unwritten contract between employers and their managers.

Why Managers Are Bitter

In and of itself, the unraveling of the contract was enough to throw middle managers into a state of shock. Mass layoffs happened to blue-collar factory workers, not them. Now the situation was reversed—unionized plant workers got more protection from layoffs than their bosses did.

Fifteen years ago, says plant worker Larry Kirk, a 26-year veteran with Cummins Engine Co., his major goal was to move up into management. But when he was eventually offered a management job in 1989, he turned it down. "It meant leaving the union—giving up all protection if there is another cutback. Now I just can't take that chance; I have to stay where I am."

But the dissolution of the unwritten contract is not alone responsible for the bitter breach between employers and their middle managers. Many managers recognize that with the inexorable forces changing the business world, the old contract could not survive in its traditional form. What ticks them off is the way they have been treated by their employers. Add to the dissolving of the contract a large dose of bad management, and you have a perfect recipe for destroying the loyalty and commitment of middle managers.

In their near-manic efforts to become lean and mean, many companies simply forgot about what they've always proclaimed was their most important asset: their employees. Instead of viewing their managers as unique individuals, employers lumped them together when they used terms like *headcount, backfill,* and *deadwood.*

This, more than anything else, is what has led today's middle managers to view their employers with distrust and suspicion—and to work in a climate of fear and anxiety.

How do they believe that management has failed them? In our interviews with middle managers who have been involved in downsizings and restructurings, we heard six major complaints over and over again:

- Lack of honest, open communication.
- Lack of recognition for accomplishments.
- Failing to treat downsized employees with respect and dignity.
- Misleading employees about future downsizings.
- Ignoring the impact of downsizing on the survivors.
- Allowing the gap between top-management and middle-management compensation to escalate beyond reasonable proportions.

Whether these perceptions are totally justified or not, they are there. These are the convictions that govern the way today's managers look at their jobs and their employers. If these convictions are to be changed to more positive attitudes, they must first be recognized and examined. That we will do in the next two chapters.

CHAPTER 2

THE THROWAWAY MANAGER: AS DISPOSABLE AS KLEENEX

I was called in at 3:30 on a Thursday afternoon and told the next day would be my last with the Hexcel Company. The severance package was two-months' salary and medical benefits. I could use the office and facilities to pursue another position—that was the outplacement. It is a day I will never forget. It undermined my whole self-esteem. It also led to five months of unemployment, the depletion of our life savings, and relocation to another state after living in the same area for nine years. It took more than 200 résumés and dozens of interviews before I found a new position. Even though I have another job, life will never be the same for me and my family. To this day, if I leave work early and get home before my family, they have an anxiety attack when they see me.
—Former production manager at a chemicals firm

With its penchant for creating euphemisms to soften unpleasant news, U.S. business has graced the downsizing era with a variety of oblique terms to describe what used to be called being fired. Among the choice phrases now in vogue are:

- Eliminating redundancies.
- Getting rid of the deadwood.
- Reducing headcount.
- Decoupling personnel.
- Outplacing personnel.

- Demassing.
- Career adjustment.

But whatever the term used, it still hurts. "Until you go through it, you don't know how what a blow it can be," one displaced manager said. "In the pain category it ranks right up there with losing a loved one, getting divorced, or being told you have an incurable disease."

Psychologically, many managers identify themselves with their job. And when they lose their job it's like losing a part of themselves. As a result, they often succumb to depression, anger, lowered self-esteem—and in extreme cases, mental illness or even suicide.

For most managers, losing their job is a loss from which they never fully recover. James Spackey, a publications manager who was let go after 17 years, wrote in *Newsweek*: "You will not be made whole again. Nothing can restore the sense of bedrock security that sustained your previous life. You will not sleep as soundly as you once slept."

Often, being downsized out of a job destroys the very underpinnings on which a manager's life is based. Dr. John Clizbe, a psychological consultant with Nordli, Wilson Asso-

---

After the Downsizing

There is a hastily organized farewell party at the local saloon to memorialize the departure of the terminees, an especially unnerving occasion when mass execution has been done on a departmental scale. Here is the surreal made flesh. The smoky air is charged with extremes of anger, weeping, and manic laughter. And though most of the condemned are suprisingly stoic, they are nonetheless wreathed with the melancholy aura that hovers about those bound for the gallows.

James Spackey, "The RIPPing of Mid-Managers," *Newsweek*, April 18, 1988, p. 10.

ciates, has counseled many displaced managers. He told us: "I think the right phrase to describe the impact is *shattered assumptions.* You have certain assumptions about the job and about yourself. You feel you know how to handle the job and that your family could always count on you to provide an income. Now those assumptions have been blown out of the water."

Anxiety and stress take their toll not only on the displaced manager but on everyone else in the household. One downsized manager describes it this way:

> The first time this happened to me, I felt resentment and anxiety. What if I couldn't find another job? But my wife was even more upset. She was concerned that I wouldn't ever be able to get anything and kept worrying about what was going to happen to us. "My God," she said one day, "here you are 56 years old and you're out of a job." The worst part was just before I got another job. My separation pay was about to run out, the outplacement facilities were no longer available, and my wife was saying, "Here we are right in the middle of the Christmas season and there's no money coming in."

BITTER HARVEST

Some displaced managers never return to the corporate world, but most do take jobs with other companies. Often, their attitudes toward work and toward employers have been profoundly changed by their trauma. What they bring to their new job is an entirely different outlook that can seriously affect their contribution to the organization. Such a negative impact can be seen in this case of a middle manager who lost his job while still in his 30s:

> After college, I worked toward my goal of becoming the operations manager at a small unit bank in Austin, Texas. My career path included moves to Houston and Corpus Christi and graduate work at three universities—while starting a family. I read all the right books, dressed for success, and managed in one minute. At 36, I was promoted to senior vice

president and cashier of Republicbank South Austin. I had it made—I thought.

I was a company man to a T. Much of my time was spent finding ways to save the company money—primarily by squeezing the most efficient return from staffing, particularly at the line-management level. Everyone's responsibilities increased to the point where we were just getting the job done without any attention toward advancing or improving the company. We were a lean machine, and I knew I had played an important role in the continuing profitability of our bank.

In January 1987, it was announced that we would be merging with our crosstown rival, Interfirst Bank, known to have serious loan portfolio deterioration problems. The new firm would be called First Republicbank Corporation. There would probably be consolidations of facilities and layoffs. Speculation and conjecture about the future became the dominating topic of conversation. Customer service and productivity suffered.

I was among a group of managers asked to participate in facilities and functions consolidation planning—for many, the blueprints for the elimination of their jobs. A seed of worry began to germinate in my head. Logically, with the impending conversion of my unit bank to a branch, my job would be scaled down or phased out. But we were assured that the valuable employees (I had received a "Star Performer" cash bonus in April) would still have a place in the company.

We all knew that the deal with Interfirst would be finalized on May 15. We also knew that some people would lose their jobs on that day. We didn't know that we, four other administrative and lending officers and myself, would be among them.

After having been dismissed like an unneeded factory worker, I developed a different outlook on working. Now I think of working as just a way to provide a better standard of living for my family. That's the outlook that keeps me motivated these days.

I think I learned two important lessons:

1. Your job isn't as important as family and friends. When you're stripped of your professional armor, you realize that your family—not career success—is your highest priority.

2. Numbers and profits have evolved into being more important than people in generating stockholder return. The larger a company gets, the easier it is to treat people as "overhead reduction opportunities."

FROM TEAM PLAYERS TO MERCENARIES

Managers who feel that their companies look at them as "overhead reduction opportunities" are likely to be motivated more by fear than anything else. The idea of committing themselves wholeheartedly to the long-range goals of their organization is the farthest thing from their minds. The closest thing is self-preservation.

Teamwork is often a victim of their changed attitude. James Guinan learned that the hard way when he tried to form a management team as new CEO of Consolidated Stores. Guinan, a turnaround specialist in retailing, had already been through two takeovers when he was hired by Consolidated to do something about its precipitous drop in pretax income. As he describes his efforts to put a management team together:

> I hired about 30 managers from outside the organization to make up my team, and for one shining year it all worked as it should, with everything jelling and profits booming. Then the predators came calling again and I soon realized that my team wasn't working together the way a management team is supposed to. It took me a while to figure out why. The answer was that they were all combat veterans of the merger and acquisition frenzy and that had entirely changed their attitudes. One had been through three takeovers in just a few years, and they all understood what might happen and that they would probably not be around to profit long-term from their efforts.
>
> So I had a hell of a time developing a team. My managers were like the mercenaries of the Middle Ages. They withheld information from each other and from me. They had an overdeveloped survival instinct which said: "Don't tell the boss

anything that's bad news." This drove me nuts, because I'm a long-leash guy and I've got to have integrity and openness from my managers. The problem was that these managers had gone down twice or more with their ships and they tended to hang around the lifeboats instead of helping to steer.

DEVELOPING A POSITIVE PERSPECTIVE

Many displaced managers are learning to adjust more positively to the unwanted changes in the business world. O. E. "Ed" Unser, the quality assurance manager we quoted in Chapter 1, for example, went through an interesting evolution as he endured displacement three times within two years:

> The first time it happened to me I felt angry and betrayed. Why was I so resentful? For one thing, I'd been recruited from the Midwest to take this job—I'd come all this way to the East Coast and now all of a sudden after seven years they didn't want me any more. Maybe it was an old-fashioned idea, but I fully expected to retire at this company. Instead, I was put out on the street. I was also angry because of the way it happened. The company had been bought by a Wall Street investment firm with the idea of selling off the most profitable plants. They incorporated my plant with another one over a thousand miles away and then sold it. They ended up making 10 times their money on the acquisition. But it cost me and 150 other employees our jobs.
>
> It took me seven months to find another job. I got a lot more spiritual during this period—I was down on my knees praying far more often than I ever was before. When I did get a job with a paper mill, it lasted just 10 months because the company that operated it decided to close it down after being threatened with a strike. But there were a couple of things that made it less traumatic. First, they provided good outplacement services and gave me salary continuance. Second, I had more confidence in my ability to get another job. In my previous job hunt, I'd gone through the whole process of personal evaluation, done a lot of reading, spoken to a lot of

people, and set up a good network. With my experience, I was actually able to help other employees of the plant find jobs. I ended up teaching at a program that a local civic group was putting on for people changing jobs after 40. Most of the people participating had never gone through the experience of losing their jobs before and were worried about being hired when they were in their 40s and early 50s. When they saw this old goat of damn near 60 walking in and saying, "Hey, I did it," they felt better. I told them how to set up networks, do résumés, market themselves.

As a result of what's happened, I've developed a new perspective. I still feel that as long as I'm performing well, I should be able to keep my job. But at least now I know that if anything happens, I can handle it. It can be frustrating and ego-shattering, but I know I can go out there and market myself. We have to face the reality that no job is permanent any more. My son is a computer scientist on his sixth job—and he's only been out of school for eight years. He doesn't even think about a job being permanent.

THE ORGANIZATION MAN (WOMAN) TAKES A WALK

Many ousted managers try to work their way back into the corporate fold—but others decide to march to a different drummer. A lot of them are starting their own businesses, and the main reason, says one outplacement executive, is worry about being downsizing victims again if they take a corporate job. Joan Learn, president of The Greenwich Group, told *Management Review,* "My clients aren't being discharged because they're incompetent. They're leaving because their companies were streamlined and simply no longer need them. That's scary, because it can happen at any firm, especially if it's another large company."

The attitude of many downsized managers toward another corporate job is "Who needs it?" One manager told us:

When I was downsized out of a job, it wasn't that traumatic—although there was much wailing and crying and gnashing of teeth by other employees who weren't as aware of what was happening. But since my last two years on the job had been sheer hell, I wasn't that upset. I had a bothersome hernia during those years, and I haven't had any problem with it since being terminated. And I don't have that tremendous anxiety. Now I'm in consulting. I'm still networking to look for another job, but I'm not going to work for any more big organizations—only a small company. No more large corporate cultures for me. I cannot stand working for people who are not honest with themselves, who don't listen to their workers, and who get so imbued with their self-importance that they forget what the business is all about.

That's a frequent refrain from displaced managers. The impact of losing their jobs has left them with an almost fearful aversion to making themselves vulnerable once again.

About 20 percent of all managers who lose their jobs now start their own firms, compared with 7 percent in 1985, according to a survey of 2,400 clients by the Chicago job search firm Challenger, Gray and Christmas.

Richard Loretta left as head of international in a major capital-goods manufacturing company to run his own firm representing American companies who want to do business in Mexico and vice versa. He told us:

My attitude toward working for a big company has changed radically because of my experience. It used to be, "Hey, that's what you're supposed to do." But now I tell my kids, "You really ought to get yourself with a good company for maybe 10 or 15 years and get the good technical experience, whether it's in finance or marketing, or whatever, and then go and do your own thing." To me, working for a large company is a necessary evil for many people, especially when you're starting out, because it enables you to learn a lot about how the business world works. Then you are in a position to go off on your own, if you want to take that route.

Attitudes like this are costing large corporations heavily. The people who feel this way are often the brightest, most experienced members of the corporate team. Many of them may not be well suited to entrepreneurial careers (according to Greenwich Group, starting their own business appeals to 7 out of 10 displaced managers, but only one in three actually takes the plunge after being told how tough it is). However, they are seasoned executives with valuable business know-how and expertise. Only their frustration and anger over conditions in the corporate world prevent them from making their talents available to a larger organization. Thus, by creating a hostile, unappealing corporate environment, companies are depriving themselves of tremendously valuable human assets.

THE EARLY RETIREMENT OPTION: A TEMPTING TRAP?

Downsizing corporations point to early retirement packages as the painless way to cut their work forces. By offering generous retirement incentives, they maintain, they can streamline their operations without having to unceremoniously fire hundreds of midlevel managers.

Does the early-retirement route soften the impact of being displaced? In many cases, yes. Undoubtedly, a sweetened early-retirement package can be extremely inviting. Employers may offer, for example, a "5–5–4" package, which adds five years to the employee's age, five to his or her service in calculating retirement benefits, and four weeks of pay per year of work as a lump sum. In late 1989 IBM offered even more generous incentives to reduce its work force, dubbed the "7, 7, and 1" package, meaning seven years would be added to the employee's age and length of service, while the employee would get a bonus of one year's pay. (Some skeptical IBM employees turned that into a "7, 7, 1, 1, and 2" program: seven years added to age, seven to service, a one-year bonus, one minute to think about it, and you have to take two people with you.)

Some middle managers have taken advantage of early retirement incentives with enthusiasm. "As far as I was concerned," said one manager who was offered a substantial retirement package, "it was a case of take the money and run."

But to other managers, the humaneness of this downsizing approach is open to question. And a large number aren't just griping about it—they're taking their former employers to court.

Their argument: Voluntary early retirement incentives aren't as voluntary as they seem. The company, they say, is putting them between a rock and a hard place by implying that if they don't take the package they'll lose their job anyway—or at least face a very uncertain future. Basically, claim the litigating managers, the company is trying to get rid of its older workers—which is illegal age discrimination.

Many of the managers we interviewed agreed. We had this dialogue with a former manager for a large maker of materials handling equipment:

Q. How did they handle the downsizing?
A. They had early retirement plans and all kinds of formulas that justified, in effect, their turning out to pasture people they didn't want.
Q. Were they picking out the older managers?
A. Yes. They were taking the convenient way to get rid of the older ones. If you were older, then you could volunteer for early retirement and they made it worth your while.
Q. What happened if you didn't volunteer?
A. Then they volunteered you.
Q. How did they do that?
A. They called you in and said you have two choices, you can volunteer for this thing or we can fire you.

WAIVING GOOD-BYE

An increasingly controversial condition of many early-retirement programs is that employees who accept the package must sign a form waiving any potential legal claim against the employers. Employers who use this device argue that it is necessary to avoid expensive age discrimination lawsuits. Employees insist that by signing the waivers they give away their legal rights even if they become convinced later that they were age discrimination victims. So far, however, appellate courts have upheld the right of employers to require the waivers as a condition for accepting the sweetened early-retirement package—so long as the employee has not been coerced into signing.

Many managers retort that requiring waivers *is* a form of coercion because they have unequal bargaining power and are under intense pressure to make up their minds. One employee for a large office-equipment company had just 11 days to decide whether to accept the early-retirement package or face the possibility of being discharged in a future layoff—in which case he would get severance pay but no benefits.

"You're in a total sweat," he remembers. "You're not thinking straight. You just don't know which way to turn." After being alerted by his boss that he would probably be let go anyway, he accepted the early-retirement package and signed the waiver. But he later joined a dozen other ex-employees in an age discrimination suit against their former employer charging that they had been replaced by younger, less well-paid employees.

Severance Pay According to Shakespeare

        . . . Take thy reward.
Five days do we allot thee for provision
To shield thee from disasters of the world,
And on the sixth to turn thy hated back
Upon our kingdom. . . .
—*King Lear*

Despite the growing legal battles over the waiver practice, more and more companies are using it. According to government data, about 80 percent of Fortune 100 companies offered an early-retirement program between 1979 and 1988. Although only 13 percent required waivers in 1983, more than 35 percent required them in 1988. And a 1989 survey by Michael Simon Associates reported that middle managers at 55 percent of the respondent companies must sign releases agreeing not to sue if they want enhanced severance benefits.

DON'T RUSH ME

Psychologically, being offered an early-retirement package can be as much of a blow to one's self-esteem as simply being terminated. Even though it seems to be a gentler approach, the message is still the same: "We don't want you any more."

For some managers this blow is softened by their lack of enthusiasm for staying on the job, anyway. If the retirement offer is generous enough, they see it as a way to get out of an unpleasant situation without sacrificing too much income.

But many managers aren't psychologically ready to stop working. They still want the mental challenge of solving problems and making decisions. That desire isn't satisfied when the toughest decision they have to make every day is whether to play golf or go shopping. Many early retirees also miss the workplace interaction and socialization of corporate life.

And if they accept an early-retirement package with the idea of continuing to work elsewhere, they soon learn that it isn't that easy. No matter how good they were at their former job, potential new employers may lack confidence that they can transfer their talents to a totally different corporate setting. Although such qualifications as flexibility should be judged on an individual basis regardless of age, many employers automatically assume that older managers cannot fit readily into a new environment.

Jim White is a volunteer at Senior Employment Resources in Annandale, Virginia, where his mission is to help some 30 early retirees—all managers or professionals 55 years old plus—get back into the job market. Success has been extremely limited, he says. His advice for those thinking of early retirement: "Don't leave your job unless they carry you out on a stretcher."

Despite its drawbacks, however, early retirement *can* be the most humane approach to downsizing.

FINDING ANOTHER JOB: WHAT ARE THE PROSPECTS?

It's no easy task for a displaced manager to find another suitable job. That's shown clearly by the results of Drake Beam Morin's 1989 Executive Outplacement Study. The outplacement firm studied 1,508 clients and came up with these conclusions:

- The length of the job hunt depends on age, salary, and type of position.
- The average length of search was 5.9 months, up from 5.1 months in 1988.
- The older the job hunter, the longer the search—averaging 6.9 months for those over 55.
- The higher the salary, the longer the search, with those making more than $100,000 also taking an average of 6.9 months to find a new position.
- Corporate staff managers took the longest to find new jobs at 7.6 months, with information system managers taking almost as long at 7.2 months.

Here's a breakdown of the survey:

	Average Length of Job Search (months)
Age	
25–34	4.8
35–44	5.7
45–54	6.6
55+	6.9
Salary	
$25,000–$39,999	5.3
$40,000–$74,999	5.8
$75,000–$99,999	5.7
$100,000+	6.9
Function	
General management	5.9
Corporate staff	7.6
Finance and accounting	6.0
Marketing and sales	5.5
Operations	5.7
Human resources	6.3
Information systems	7.2
Engineering	5.3
Science	4.5
Other	5.7
Gender	
Women	5.3
Men	6.0

Source: The 1989 Drake Beam Morin Executive Outplacement Study.
Reprinted from National Business Employment Weekly, August 27, 1989.

One development that makes it easier for displaced managers to find employment is a change in attitude toward those who are let go. The ongoing massive downsizing of U.S. corporations has helped to remove much of the stigma from being unemployed in midcareer. For example, executive-search consultants keep themselves informed about large companies that are undergoing restructuring and provide pools of men and women who want or need to pursue second and third careers. The bad news is that by the late 1980s, the supply of middle and senior managers far exceeded the demand, particularly for general managers. With many companies removing entire layers of management, there is simply not room enough for all the general

What about the Poor Abused Employer?

One employer decided to mount a counteroffensive after reading an article in *Business Week* about dismissed workers who were filing lawsuits against their ex-employers. Jeffrey B. McLaughlin, president of the Norton-Murphy Sales Corporation (Dayton, N.J.), wrote to the editor:

> I have a modest proposal. Employees leave all the time. Let's start to sue them. Let's fill the courts with backlogged cases by aggrieved employers who have had less-than-adequate warning that an employee is leaving.
>
> Employees talk to employment agencies and headhunters on our time and on our phones. They use our typewriters, our word processors, and our nonletterhead stationery to create their résumés. They use our manila envelopes and stamps. They call in sick or are absent to attend interviews. In most cases, they demand compensation for vacations and sick days not used. To add insult to injury, they use us as a reference. And they leave with our training, our business plans, and our customer lists.
>
> Let's sue them to recover the costs of training their replacements; sue them to recover the agency fees we paid; sue them to recover the cost of the health plans, insurance, pension plans, etc. that we have to administer to attract them.
>
> The next time one of your employees says he or she is leaving for a better job, tell them: "I'll see you in court." If business can't fire at will, then an employee should not be able to leave at will.

So far, the record does not show that any employers have heeded Mr. McLaughlin's battle cry.

Business Week, November 21, 1988.

managers who have been displaced. (This is also shown by the fact that reemployed general managers, on average, settle for new salaries lower than their old ones.) Jerry Simmons, president of Handy Associates, told us in the spring of 1989: "I have never seen so much available talent out there." Other executive-search consultants confirmed this condition, as does the continued growth of the outplacement industry.

Forging a second career or even finding a suitable job is not always easy for victims of restructurings. Typically, outplaced managers initially find themselves at a loss—psychologically and practically. Many of them were recruited at college and stayed with their employer of first choice until they were prematurely terminated. Having never written a résumé in their lives, they begin with this task. As a result, executive-search firms receive thousands of résumés each week. But these firms are employed by client companies that seek to fill specific jobs, so the probability of finding a job by sending unsolicited résumés to executive-search firms is slim.

For managers whose former employers provide outplacement services, support is available. But it is only support. It is still the manager's task to find his or her own job, calling on networks of friends and acquaintances, conducting research on industries in which they have worked, and so on. For many suddenly unemployed managers there are no outplacement services, no employer facilities available, no place to go from nine to five. They must work out of their homes, creating card indexes, crossing out name after name from a yellow-pad listing of potentially helpful contacts. Finding a way to that second or third—or fourth—career can be a lonely and often frustrating job.

However, networks of groups have sprung up to share techniques and provide psychological support. The *National Business Employment Weekly,* published by *The Wall Street Journal,* carries a biweekly calendar of events listed "to publicize events and services for job seekers that are either free or of nominal cost." A mid-June 1989 issue, for example, listed 80 events, ranging from meetings of for-profit career consultants to church-based organizations. One long-established group is the Forty-Plus Club, a national organization with some 15 U.S. locations. Among available books, one of the most useful is *What Color Is Your Parachute?* by Richard N. Bolles.

As we head into the 1990s, there would seem to be brighter prospects for displaced managers who are searching for new jobs. All signs point to a growing scarcity of managerial talent as work force growth slows down.

THE REAL COST OF DOWNSIZING

The cost of frantic, ill-planned downsizing is not borne only by those who lose their jobs. Eventually, they will find other jobs or other careers. But the impact of being displaced leaves a bitter residue that will not go away. It will be with these people when they take their next job and will drastically affect their attitudes toward their employer. Some of the brightest will never return to the corporate world—they will go off in their own directions as consultants and entrepreneurs. U.S. business will thus lose some of its outstanding managerial talent when it most desperately needs it.

And what about the survivors—the managers who escape the axe and remain to cope with a very different organization from what they have always known? We shall take up their plight in the next chapter.

CHAPTER 3

SURVIVOR SYNDROME: FEAR AND ANXIETY AT THE WATER COOLER

Because of our constant downsizings, rumors were always flying around like crazy. When you saw people gathered in the hall, you knew they weren't talking about work—they were speculating about the next bloodbath. Every discussion was a never-ending bitch-and-gripe session.
—Survivor in a major beauty products firm

After a massive downsizing, the survivors must carry on. They must shoulder greater responsibilities and perform increasingly complex tasks to keep the organizational wheels turning. Making it possible for them to do this effectively is among the most urgent challenges facing employers today.

It is mind-boggling, then, that so many companies neglect the serious problems that survivors of downsizing face in adjusting to the traumatic event itself and to the new conditions in which they must now work. Although some forward-looking firms are beginning to pay more attention to survivors, few of the companies we researched did anything to help them cope. One middle manager in a medical services firm complained, "The survivors of our downsizing were basically ignored by senior management, who felt they were busy with more important tasks." A human resources manager for a major oil company conceded that although her firm was very solicitous about the employees who were being let go, it did nothing to deal with the problems faced by those who remained.

Behind this failure to deal with survivor syndrome are several common corporate attitudes:

- "No problem exists."
- "We're too busy with the important part of reorganization: financial details."
- "Time will take care of it."
- "They should feel lucky they still have jobs."

Whatever the reason for neglecting survivor problems, the result is often a demoralized managerial work force. The problems associated with such demoralization are many, complex, and not easily solved. One of them is survivor shock.

SURVIVOR SHOCK

Even those employees who are still at their desks when the dust settles are shocked by the downsizing experience. True, they may be thankful that they still have jobs. But that relief is tempered by the grim realization that if their friends and colleagues can be abruptly handed pink slips, they can too. "You realize that life will never be the same," one manager in a chemicals firm explained. "The family you've grown used to has broken up and disappeared. Somehow you feel that you've lost your moorings and you're far more vulnerable than you were before."

From his extensive experience in counseling downsizing survivors, John Clizbe, a management psychologist with Nordli, Wilson Associates, believes that the stressful impact on middle managers is perhaps more severe than on any other level of the organization:

> They usually get a little bit of information but not enough to feel that they can really do anything about it. Everything

seems totally out of their control. They feel no ability to influence anything that's happening—instead, they're completely dependent on whoever is doing the negotiations or
planning the work force reductions. Another factor that creates stress is how important their jobs are to them. The
middle-level manager probably feels a greater need for his or
her job than the top-level officers. The top executive assumes,
"I'm going to be protected by a golden parachute so it will all
work out okay." But the middle-level manager feels a high degree of insecurity. Often these mergers and acquisitions and
downsizings occur in smaller towns where the company is the
main employer, and if you're not working for that employer,
there aren't too many jobs available in the area for you to go
to. So it's a problem for middle managers, who often have
their roots in the town and their kids going to high school.
That's another source of stress—it's just very important for
them to keep their jobs.

When security is replaced by insecurity, fear becomes a
dominant emotion. After AT&T pared 25,000 employees
from its work force in 1989, Joel Gross, a telecommunications analyst with Donaldson Lufkin & Jenrette, commented: "All the employees are optimistic about the
company, but at the same time they are scared out of their
minds about their jobs." It seems that their fear was justified. At the end of the year, the company announced that it
would cut another 8,500 jobs in 1990.

The Impact of Disaster

Extensive research into survivor syndrome reveals strong
similarities between the reactions of downsizing survivors
and survivors of such disasters as earthquakes, plane
crashes, the Hiroshima bomb, and the Nazi death camps.
The symptoms are the same: a combination of relief, guilt,
anger, and anxiety.

For psychologist John Clizbe, the universality of survivor syndrome hit home when a tornado devastated a neigh-
borhood near his New Haven, Connecticut, home in 1989:

When I read about the reactions of people to that tragedy, I saw a lot of parallels to what survivors experience after a downsizing. The initial reaction was a sense of relief: "OK, our house collapsed around us, but we're alive." I think the same thing happens in organizations. "The house of cards has collapsed, but I'm still alive, I'm still here in the organization." So there's an initial sense of relief that's very understandable.

But the feeling of relief is only temporary. It's followed by a period of mourning over the loss—the fact that the person who sat in the next office to yours is now gone. People have to do that mourning—if management tries to shut it off too quickly, the result will be some serious psychological or even physiological aftereffects.

The third stage is anxiety. "OK, they got rid of 200 people, but are they going to discover next week that they should have gotten rid of 250?" There's a tremendous amount of insecurity about their own personal status.

Another feeling is guilt. "How come I made it and the guy next to me didn't?"

The next thing that happens is a diminished sense of trust. All the old assumptions, all the implied contracts, don't seem to exist any more. "I've got to protect myself." This is probably one of the most lasting aftereffects of a downsizing. Surviving managers go through a lot of reality testing, where they're checking to find out if they can trust management. If they decide the answer is no, there's a real loss of loyalty, commitment, trust, credibility, and communication. What happens then is that the survivors become much more cautious about what they say. For example, "If I tell my boss that I forgot to do something or if I let him know that I took a risk and it didn't pan out, am I going to be in deep trouble?"

Seething Underneath the Surface: Anger

For obvious reasons, most surviving managers will not openly express their anger at top management, except to each other. One survivor described his reaction to a downsizing this way:

> I was a middle manager for a small division with line authority for operations in the western half of the United States.

Just before taking a week off to attend a management course, I asked my superior how I was performing. He told me I was "doing just great." When I got back from the course, I discovered that several layers of management and numerous positions had been eliminated, including my own. As my performance was not in question, I was retained in a lesser position. Like many of the survivors, I was angry at top management for what happened. We thought that management had brought about the conditions that required the restructuring, but had not shared the burden as they should have. Senior management was totally unaffected except for one vice president who was on leave and returned to find her position had disappeared. Some of the poorer performers in senior management kept their jobs. For many of the survivors, the feeling about the company was definitely changed. They were much more wary in trusting the company to keep their welfare in mind.

A data processing manager with a high-tech firm doing business with the Pentagon puts it even more strongly. After several downsizings, he reported, the attitude of survivors toward the company became totally negative:

I never saw so much anxiety, anger, poor morale, and hatred for top management. It permeated the work environment and made it difficult for the survivors to perform their responsibilities. Employee respect for the company has been eliminated by top management's inability to communicate properly. It seems they just stuck their heads in the sand during the downsizings. There is not a day that goes by without an employee asking me why a certain employee was laid off.

Guilt Trip

Along with relief over keeping one's job goes guilt that others lost theirs. "It took me a long time to get over my guilt feelings," said one survivor in a large publishing firm. "When co-workers you've known for 10 years are suddenly put out on the street, you almost feel like walking out with them in protest. But you don't—and that makes the guilt feelings even worse."

Guilt feelings increase when survivors see that many of those employees who were dismissed were performing as well as they were. The human resources manager of a mid-size manufacturer said:

> My company has gone through one reduction a year for the past four years. We started off by terminating the poor performers, and this didn't seem to upset the morale of the survivors very much. But by the third year we'd already gotten rid of the deadwood, and it reached the point where if you were in the wrong place at the wrong time you could be fired no matter what a great performer you were. It was simply a situation where we needed to take X number of people out of the business or we wouldn't be in the business any more. That's what really turned the place upside down—and morale now has hit bottom.

Unfortunately, says psychological consultant David M. Noer, very few companies help their survivors cope with their feelings of anger, guilt, anxiety, and depression. "On the contrary," he says, "management usually ignores these feelings—which is a form of denial that they exist."

A basic problem, contends Noer, is that companies no longer perceive employees as assets to be developed but as costs to be reduced. The language of downsizing is the language of numbers: "We reduced headcount by 2,000 last year."

Noer summarizes the typical senior management speech to the remaining troops this way: "I know a lot of people have left, but you've got to understand that our ROI wasn't sufficient to get the stock up, and since the stock wasn't up, earnings per share dropped, etc."

The trouble with that approach, says Noer, is that management doesn't acknowledge that people have been wounded and are in no mood to listen to numbers.

OVERWORKED AND UNDERAPPRECIATED

When a company shrinks, the amount of work to be done seldom shrinks with it. So now the same amount of work has to be done by fewer people. And that's a sore point with many downsizing survivors. Richard Chagnon, a senior corporate executive in Right Associates, one of the nation's largest outplacement firms, puts it this way:

> For example, take a company of 1,200 people that's just been downsized to 800. These 800 people are loyal, hard workers who are now trying to do what the 1,200 did. And therein lies the problem. The perception of the structure and workload of the company didn't really change. All that happened was that the headcount was reduced. Everyone is still trying to do what used to be done when the company was 1,200 strong. The survivors are working longer days, their salaries have probably been frozen, and management is counting on their loyalty to pull the company through. Obviously, this is a formula for failure. Your workers will get caught in a web of conflicting emotions: guilt and anger, frustration and discouragement.

Many surviving managers end up with job descriptions that double their responsibilities. Their salaries don't go up commensurately, however. And there are days when they wonder if they are too overloaded to adequately discharge their managerial responsibilities. One survivor at General Electric's Medical Systems Group told *Business Week*:

> Quite honestly, I feel overworked. I work hard, and sometimes I don't enjoy it anymore. Before the delayering last October, I had a total of 10 people who would report to me, and 4 of them were other managers who had people reporting to them. After that, I wound up with 20 people. I'm usually here at 7 A.M. and I leave at 6 at night—about 55 hours a week.
> It just seems like it gets busier and busier and busier. The other day, one of my managers walked up to me, put out his hand, and said: "Hi, remember me? I work for you." That's part of the problem, you don't see as much of your people. That makes me feel bad as a manager.

Along with the increased work load goes the feeling of downsizing survivors that management doesn't appreciate the efforts they are making. One survivor in a large retailing organization described his feelings:

> Salary's not everything—what would give me more satisfaction and increase my commitment would be true recognition. After our downsizing, when the pressure was on to cut costs, I saved the company almost a million dollars in a year by reducing excess catalog production. I got a little article in the company paper and that was it. After that my attitude toward management could be summed up as, "Well, screw you."

THE COLLAPSE OF THE CAREER LADDER

When a company downsizes, whole layers of management may vanish into thin air—and with them the promotional opportunities they represent to managers on lower levels. "For the survivors, there are no opportunities," said one 30-year-old manager. "Moving up is a thing of the past." This reality can have an intensely demoralizing impact on those managers who entered the job market with visions of a steady, almost guaranteed climb up the corporate ladder.

To most managers, progress means promotion. This is why companies in the 50s and 60s made sure there were plenty of ranks and grades to be promoted to, even if the differences in level were really insignificant except as a mechanism for granting pay increases. Slow, but steady, progress upward is what sustained many managers, rather than the intrinsic interest of the job they were doing.

Then came restructuring, and the corporate ladder collapsed along with the organization chart. This virtually took away the incentive that had kept many managers performing their jobs—and they were not happy about it. "I'm at a dead end," said one manager. "There's no way up. No way down. And no way out."

TURNING OFF THE MONEY SPIGOT

Traditionally, salary increases for middle managers have been based on promotions. Although every position has a salary range, once you are at the top of the range your only way to get more money is to be promoted. That is one reason so many layers of management were built into the organization.

When those layers are eliminated in a downsizing, the surviving managers suddenly find that their heads are jammed up against a monetary ceiling. Not only are they unable to move upward to the next salary range, but they are also unlikely to get a pay raise in their current range, or they may even suffer a pay cut as their employers tighten up on costs.

The reasonableness of their expectations for steady upgrades in compensation is open to debate. After all, the traditional pay-and-hierarchy formula doesn't necessarily produce highly motivated achievers. Its implied guarantee of monetary progress has never been closely tied to actual job performance. Even mediocre performers are rewarded with pay boosts.

But middle managers are not responsible for creating the pay-and-hierarchy system. It was created by corporations who demanded long-term loyalty from their managers and secured that loyalty by promising steady pay increases as they climbed up through the organization chart. As one human resources manager in a huge oil company put it: "We had a very parental relationship with our managers. We never really played hardball with the weaker managers—and in pay raises they didn't fare much differently than outstanding performers."

Regardless of the deficiencies of the pay-and-hierarchy system, however, it *was* the system. And when widespread downsizings and restructurings made it unworkable, another managerial assumption was shattered, adding to the feeling of betrayal and bitterness among surviving managers.

MEANWHILE, IN THE
EXECUTIVE SUITE ...

Surviving managers found no solace when they compared what was happening to their pay to what was happening to top executive pay. While middle managers had to tighten their belts, top management faced no such requirement. The pressure for cutting costs seemed to stop at the doors to the executive suite. Between salaries, bonuses, stock options, stock grants, restricted stock, and increased cash payouts, executive pay accelerated like a rocket during the 1980s, while middle management pay increases slowed to a trickle. Average total CEO pay was $624,999 in 1980—by 1989 it was nearly $1.9 million. That was about 90 times the average pay of a factory worker. In 1960 average CEO pay was 41 times that of the average factory worker.

Meanwhile, middle management pay in the 1980s was creeping up at about 5 percent a year—a manager making $30,000 in 1980 would be making slightly less than $50,000 by 1989—in cheaper dollars. It is no secret to most surviving managers that the gap between their pay and the pay of top executives has been widening every year. For example, the Hay Group reported that salaries and bonuses paid in 1988 to chief executives at 231 large and medium-sized industrial companies surged an average of 17.4 percent. Only in 1989 did that pace slow down—and many observers considered this an aberration.

Top executive perks are also a source of irritation for many middle managers. While top management proclaims the need for cutting costs to the bone, that philosophy doesn't seem to apply to things like luxurious corporate aircraft and other amenities of the executive life. For example, when First Interstate Bancorp's chairman and chief executive Joseph Pinola installed stringent cost controls, one manager responded by dropping the bank's reserved valet parking spots at the Hollywood Bowl entertainment center. When he found out, Pinola ordered the parking spots restored. According to a former colleague, "He didn't think that walking from the cheap parking lot past all the other bankers' limousines befit him."

When F. Ross Johnson was chairman of RJR Nabisco, a frequent passenger on RJR private jets was listed as "G. Shepard"—and G. Shepard was always the *only* passenger. After Kohlberg Kravis Roberts took over the company in 1989, it learned that "G. Shepard" was Johnson's dog—who traveled separately because of a tendency to bite other passengers.

A middle manager who survived three downsizings at a major consumer products firm told us:

> The CEO froze wages, doubled individual workload, took away secretarial/administrative help, rescinded the annual bonus, and discontinued the free annual physical. Meanwhile, he enjoyed a private jet, a million dollar *pied à terre* in Manhattan, and a platinum parachute contract.

It's not difficult to figure out that such top management excesses don't do much for the morale of middle managers. Some of the milder words they use to describe this behavior are *greedy, unfair,* and *hypocritical.* In his book, *The Frontiers of Management,* Peter Drucker quotes one engineering manager for a large defense contractor:

> While our salary increases last year were held to 3 percent with the argument that any more would be inflationary, the nine people in the top management group voted themselves bonuses and additional stock options amounting to a 25 percent to 30 percent increase in their compensation—and that's simply dishonest.

What particularly irks managerial survivors is that very little of top executive pay is tied to performance. A 1989 analysis of compensation patterns of the 70 top executives in 439 corporations found that only 10 percent of their wages were related to changes in corporate profits, sales, or assets. Dr. Jonathan Leonard, professor in the Schools of Business and Industrial Relations at the University of California, who did the survey, commented: "Executive compensation has become all reward, no risk. Bonus pay that never changes is really just base pay under a different guise." As a case in point: The top three executives of McCaw Cellular Communications racked up a total of $92.7 million in compensation in 1989—the same year the company lost $289 million.

So when downsizing survivors have a chance to look up from their desks, the bigger picture they see is this: In their new "mean and lean" organization they get more work and more responsibilities, but their compensation doesn't reflect that. Meanwhile, their top bosses enjoy an overflowing cornucopia of expensive goodies—regardless of performance. These goodies include huge golden parachutes, such as the $53.8 million for Ross Johnson and RJR's former vice chairman, T. A. Hoorigan.

Small wonder, then, that downsizing survivors react with anger and skepticism to top-management pep talks urging them to give their all to help beat the competition.

WHERE HAVE ALL THE BENEFITS GONE?

In addition to steady promotions and raises, the old unwritten employment contract promised middle managers an array of benefits that could truly be called a security blanket. In most companies, managers received generous medical and hospital benefits entirely paid for by their employers. And through defined-benefit pension programs, they were able to plan their retirement knowing exactly how much they would have to live on after they quit working. Not only that, their postretirement benefits often included health insurance, even dental insurance. "Our employers made us very dependent," said one manager for a large farm-equipment company. "They bound us with 'golden handcuffs.' " The benefits package provided another strong incentive for managers to remain loyal and committed to their companies.

Then came the downsizing onslaught. Along with work forces, benefits shrank too. At the same time that employers became preoccupied with cutting costs, the costs of health insurance were skyrocketing. A survey by the Wyatt Company, a benefits consulting firm, showed that for 2,271 *employers* medical claims rose 13 percent in 1988, averaging $1,568 per employee, excluding dental costs and health costs for retirees. Another survey of 1,600 employers by A. Foster Higgins & Company, found that total health costs for *employers and workers combined* had risen 19 percent in 1988 alone, and 43 percent in just four years, to $2,354 per employee in 1988, including dental and retiree expenses.

The impact of these rising costs was to destroy another clause in the old unwritten employment contract. No longer did employers feel they could bear the entire burden of paying for employee health care—more and more started requiring employees to pay a greater share of the expenses. Another Wyatt Company survey found that in 1988 the percentage of employers with plans that pay 100 percent of hospital bills had fallen to 34 percent, from *69 percent* in 1978. And about 40 percent of employers planned to change health-care commitments to retirees by reducing coverage, increasing retiree contributions, or both. That was up from 20 percent just two years before.

Surviving managers are seeing their postretirement security blanket being ripped to shreds. For example, in 1988 Metropolitan Life Insurance Company sharply increased health insurance deductibles for retirees. The legality of their action was upheld, *despite promises in company newsletters of "lifetime" benefits "at no cost."* General Motors Corporation announced in 1987 that it would cut benefits for about 80,000 retirees.

Corporations today are making a sharp break with the pattern of firm commitments that they once made to their retired workers. On September 12, 1989, for example, the

New York Times reported that AT&T substantially limited spending for retiree health care in the 1990s. The effect of the plan, which was worked out with the company's unions, was to shift responsibility for financing any inflationary increases in medical costs to the future retirees.

Survivors of takeovers and mergers are particularly vulnerable to benefits cuts. As Peter Kelly, a Chicago lawyer and benefits expert, pointed out to *The Wall Street Journal*, new managements are less sensitive to the nuances of promises made by old managements. Moreover, debt acquired during a highly leveraged buyout often makes it difficult for the company to back such promises.

"At our company, we looked forward to retiring on a company-paid health insurance plan," said one survivor of a major downsizing in a cosmetics company. "Then came the bad news. We would be the ones who would be doing more and more of the paying. The company reneged on its commitment to retirees."

Predictable pension income is also a thing of the past, say many benefits experts. Defined-benefits programs are being displaced by defined-contribution programs such as 401(k) savings plans, in which employees set aside a percentage of their pretax salary with the employer matching the employee's contribution.

Most surviving managers understand that their employers are caught between the increasingly steep rises in benefits costs and the desire of their employees for total commitment to benefits of the past. Despite that understanding, however, they still feel resentful and betrayed. Many of them say:

- Employers are reneging on commitments they have already made to their employees—or in the case of takeovers and mergers, the new managements are not keeping the promises made by the old managements.

- Rather than trying to devise ways to reduce the costs of health care and pension benefits, companies are simply shifting the costs to the backs of their employees and retirees.
- Meanwhile, in the executive suite the company officers are hanging on to all the benefits and perks they have always enjoyed—indeed, they're adding to them.

MAJOR CASUALTY: COMPANY LOYALTY

What is the message being sent to corporate employers by downsizing survivors? Basically this: "Loyalty is a two-way street—and since we no longer believe you have loyalty to us, we don't feel that we owe it to you."

This attitude is borne out not only by our interviews with surviving managers but by surveys and studies. Some examples:

- A 1989 survey of 400 managers by Carnegie Mellon researcher Robert Kelley found that fully one third of them distrust their own direct bosses and 55 percent don't believe top management.
- A 1986 survey done for *Business Week* by Louis Harris & Associates showed a dramatic drop in the loyalty of middle managers to their employers. Middle managers in 600 corporations were asked, "Compared with 10 years ago, do you feel that salaried employees are more loyal, less loyal, or about as loyal as they were back then?" A majority of 65 percent answered, "Less loyal." Only 5 percent said "More loyal," while 29 percent said "About as loyal."
- A 1988 study of 1,200 middle managers by the National Institute of Business Management revealed widespread dissatisfaction. More than a third said they would probably be happier elsewhere.
- A 1989 survey of managers by the Center for Organizational Effectiveness showed that less than half of

male managers and only one in five female managers think their companies have their best interests in mind.

What's the bottom line here? It's simply that survivor managers and their employers just are not operating on the same wavelength. Although downsizing is often intended to eliminate layers and bring middle management closer to top management, this result only happens on the organization chart. Psychologically and emotionally, downsizing often creates a yawning gap between surviving managers and top executives. The bonds that were established by the old employment contract have snapped.

Most managers are basically responsible and continue to do their jobs. If there's a meeting with their customer, they have it. If there's a project to be worked on, they work on it.

But commonness of purpose has largely evaporated. A major effect of downsizing on surviving managers is to narrow their vision down to their own personal security and their own specific job tasks. They are not as concerned with corporate goals, with linking their own activities with other parts of the organization, or keeping those other units informed on matters that might affect them.

What does this do to organizational performance? Companies that believe they can downsize without regard for the impact on both laid-off managers and survivors often do not realize that they will pay a cost too. In the next chapter, we'll explore the negative impacts of downsizing on the organization.

CHAPTER 4

LEANER AND MEANER:
BUT AT WHAT PRICE?

A CEO calls his middle managers to a meeting on the company grounds. After making a short speech about the need for running "mean and lean," he gives a signal and a firing squad dispatches 15 percent of the assembled managers. Six months later he calls the survivors out again and another 15 percent are similarly eliminated. To those who are left, the CEO then says: "OK, now let's go out and kill the competition."
—Business writer John Thackrey

Extreme though it may be, Thackrey's fable underscores a dangerous trend in American business thinking today: that simply by downsizing its work force and "getting rid of the deadwood" a company can achieve a competitive edge.

It doesn't necessarily work that way. Too often, a company loses valuable talent when it downsizes, ending up even worse equipped to compete effectively than it was before. Add the huge human cost of poorly implemented downsizings, and you have both individuals and organizations paying a tremendous price for achieving very little beside short-term economies. As Robert Tomasko points out, eliminating jobs does not by itself expand markets, develop better products, provide better service, improve workers' morale, or modernize plants.

Organizational streamlining is undoubtedly an imperative for many companies, both to cut costs and to improve efficiency and flexibility. Some mergers and acquisitions *can* produce a synergistic effect that enhances total performance. But too many restructurings not only fail to reach their objectives but also actually leave the organization considerably weaker.

It's tempting to say, "We've eliminated two layers of management so we'll be more productive." Actually, a company may become a lot less productive unless it trains people in the skills they'll need and gives them some reasons for doing their best.

Then there's, "Now we've got one person for every $1,000 in sales instead of two, so obviously we're more productive." Not necessarily, because a year from now a company may have $250 in sales for every employee if it has cut out half of its technical expertise or hasn't retrained people to handle multiple responsibilities. It's unfortunate that sometimes top management is so proud of the millions it has saved by reducing headcount, it doesn't want to spoil things by investing in the people who remain.

Let's look at the negative impacts that downsizing can have on an organization's performance and ability to compete.

THE DOWNSIDE OF DOWNSIZING

The human costs of downsizing described in Chapters 2 and 3 are not necessarily uppermost in the minds of corporate leaders, who are focused on short-term financial results. But there is another downside that is more likely to get their attention: the cost to the organization.

This cost takes two major forms: first, the impact of low morale, lessened commitment, stress, and anxiety; and second, the impact of work force reductions on the ability of the organization to function efficiently and maintain a high quality of service to the customer.

The Demoralized Work Force

A majority of the people we interviewed reported that the low morale and high anxiety caused by downsizing affected the performance of remaining employees. These are some of the things they told us:

- Survivors kept a low profile and tried to merge into the woodwork. Although they did their jobs, they tended to avoid risk taking and innovation.
- Stress and anxiety took a heavy toll on performance— even to the point of increased employee illness.
- Less attention was paid to work than to discussing what was going to happen next.
- Employee loyalty and commitment evaporated, to be replaced by a climate of suspicion and skepticism in which productivity suffered sharply.
- Some survivors were busier looking for new jobs than they were working on their current ones.

The Impact on Organizational Performance

Although downsizing can undoubtedly benefit organizational effectiveness, it takes a lot more than simply firing people to produce that benefit. Many companies see their mission as reducing headcount while overlooking equally important imperatives (which we will discuss later). These companies end up with serious operational problems that can exert long-lasting effects on performance. Four of these problems are:

1. *The company can lose some of its most experienced, valuable employees*—people with company-specific skills that are difficult to replace. In some cases, more managers than expected accept a sweetened early-retirement package. A senior manager in a computer consultant firm believes

Downsizing: Hazardous to Your Health?

One middle manager in a major airline company that had been taken over and subjected to substantial downsizing reported that the number of employees with illnesses such as ulcers rose dramatically. He himself was seriously affected:

I went through a period of four months where I reported to three different senior corporate officers, each one having either resigned or lost his job—and for a period of at least three weeks I was really reporting to no one and was not sure (except that my check kept coming) whether I had a job. The stress was tremendous. I'm one of these people who usually is asleep three minutes after my head hits the pillow—but during this period I not only could not sleep most of the time, but when I did I had nightmares. Naturally, my job performance suffered. Eventually, I had to ask my doctor to prescribe medication to help me sleep.

that IBM's downsizings during the 1980s show what can go wrong with early-retirement programs.

When IBM offered an early-retirement plan, a lot of seasoned veterans suddenly became qualified for full retirement benefits. These were branch managers and area managers with 30 years at IBM and all the polish one would expect of an IBM salesperson. They opted in bunches for the early-retirement plan. IBM simply did not anticipate the ultimate effect on the organization. It was left seriously deficient in the middle sales management ranks, and that is reflected in its bottom line today. It now has a sales organization that is significantly younger, not as prepared and seasoned as it used to be.

This illustrates one of the major pitfalls of offering early-retirement packages, since by law they must be offered to all employees in a given job category or age group—and these employees must have a totally free choice. Often the first employees to take the money and run are precisely those the company wants to keep. To reduce these defections, many companies adopt some not-so-subtle ways to obliquely get a message to the employees they want to keep and those they don't—such as holding a career seminar and telling some employees they needn't attend. But the uncertain results of early-retirement incentives have led some companies to avoid them. The American Management Association's 1989 survey on downsizing found that the companies offering early-retirement packages to exempt employees during a downsizing had dropped to 32 percent from 44 percent in 1987, and those offering such programs to nonexempt employees had dropped from 31 percent to 23 percent.

Even without early-retirement incentives, however, many top performers may jump ship anyway during and after a downsizing. They can find other jobs more easily than mediocre employees, who tend to hang on for dear life. Managers with large sums in deferred compensation may just pick up and leave, since they can make almost as much money as they did from the job. The company is thus left with a shortage of the superior talent it needs to be competitive. One manager reported that in his company downsizing had some unexpected—and unwelcome—results:

> When we offered a good severance package, many of our better people actually volunteered to go. They came forward and said, "Give me a package and I'll be glad to get out of this place." Meanwhile, the drones were busily burying themselves in corners where you could never find them. In the end, we were left with a high percentage of mediocre people.

2. *Indiscriminate work force cuts can leave some essential functions understaffed and unable to provide the necessary quality of service and production.* Leanness is not a virtue in itself. One company's fat may be another company's muscle—and a company that unselectively eliminates management layers may find that it has seriously weakened itself. Hewlett-Packard, for example, found that it had to add missing layers of management to improve communication and coordination among its decentralized product divisions.

(However, it was careful to survey its employees to make sure that the new layers did not isolate them from top management.)

After the 1989 Valdez oil spill, some observers wondered if Exxon's ability to react swiftly to the disaster had been hampered by its drastic work force cuts (over 80,000 jobs since 1982). According to the *New York Times:*

> Exxon seemed to respond to the oil spill off the Alaskan coast in slow motion, raising questions of whether all the downsizing had yielded a new, improved Exxon, or had in fact weakened the company—not only in terms of a decimated oil spill control team, but of overall management control.

Another major oil spill in New York Harbor's Arthur Kill in 1990 raised new questions about whether Exxon's restructuring had stretched the company's work force too thin. Employees said the system was undermanned and overworked, and even some Exxon executives conceded that some operations were 10 percent short on personnel. Many of the personnel wiped out by broad cutbacks were managers with crucial specialized skills.

3. *Distractions caused by the turmoil of restructuring and takeover threats can erode organizational performance.* When the hectic pace of corporate change creates a climate of uncertainty and instability, management tends to lose focus on running the business. Downsizing and other types of restructuring can be harmfully disruptive. And restructuring related to the threat of takeover can be doubly distracting, particularly to the chief executive.

That point is made with some feeling by James M. Guinan, former chief executive officer of Consolidated Stores, Caldor, and Gold Circle, who describes himself as a "two-time combat veteran of the merger and acquisition frenzy":

> The threat of being acquired bursts on a company with all the subtlety of an H-bomb, particularly for a CEO. Lawyers and investment advisors flock about you, with their meters

running. Your board of directors becomes prickly and divisive. Your subordinates devote their time and energy to speculation and telephone calls to headhunters. Your direct reports replace their normal smiles for you with speculative/evaluative stares, and you spend great chunks of time on The Issue instead of business—all while that business begins to majestically unpeel.

That the distractions of restructurings and takeover threats can seriously affect organizational performance is illustrated by the experience of Avon Products, Inc. In late 1989, Avon—which had drastically downsized in the previous two years—announced that its advance sales in the United States were dropping precipitously, which meant their Christmas season would be a bust. Mystified, senior management investigated. The answer they came up with was simple: Their Christmas line cost too much.

CEO James Preston blamed the problem on restructuring and the many takeover threats with which Avon had been grappling. As more expensive products were introduced, "the people in our marketing area didn't notice the price rise," he said. And he himself had not been as involved in the operation of the business because he was too busy fighting off takeover threats from Amway Corporation, Mary Kay Cosmetics, and Minneapolis investor Irwin L. Jacobs. "You have to remember," Preston said, "that a lot of things have been going on over here. It's just a different environment." Evidently not one conducive to running an effective business.

4. *In the cost-cutting frenzy, long-term concerns are often ignored.* The ax may fall on research and development (R&D), training services, and other functions considered peripheral to short-term results. In the case of leveraged buyouts, funds are diverted from these functions to pay huge debt-servicing costs.

Research and development is an area particularly sensitive to the impact of downsizing and LBOs. The rise in U.S. corporate outlays for R&D has slowed down to 3 percent annually since 1984, half the pace of the 1970s. In early 1990, the *New York Times* reported that for the first time in 14 years, spending on corporate research and development has not even kept pace with inflation. According to a report by the National Science Foundation, R&D spending rose to $68.8 billion in 1989 from $66.5 billion in 1988. But when this increase is adjusted for inflation, it actually represents a drop of nine tenths of 1 percent. Contrast that with Japan, where the increase in R&D spending has been consistently more than three times that for U.S. companies.

Observers attributed this decline to a variety of factors, including an increasing focus by corporate managers on short-term profitability and the cost-cutting that goes along with restructurings, mergers, and leveraged buyouts.

William J. Spencer, Xerox Corporation's executive vice president for research and development, pointed out a radical change in attitude toward the R&D function. "We've moved from considering research and development as a corporate asset to where it's what corporate raiders look for first," he said. "They can make significant cuts and get cash flow. I haven't seen a takeover yet where they increased research and development activities."

Duracell, Inc., a battery maker, offers a case in point. In 1988 Duracell was acquired by Duracell Holdings Corporation in a leveraged buyout arranged by Kohlberg Kravis Roberts. The prospectus issued for the buyout pointed out that because the company would incur a heavy debt-servicing load, it might not be able "to respond adequately to technological developments." And this is a company where the ability to compete is largely based on technological advances!

Prime Computer, Inc., is another example of a company that may have been severely wounded by a leveraged buyout. After being acquired by J. H. Whitney & Co. for $1.3 billion in cash and junk bonds, it announced that it was slashing its work force by 20 percent—from 11,800 to 9,300. The reason: its staggering debt-service obligations. According to *The Wall Street Journal,* Prime made it clear that it wouldn't continue investments where it didn't foresee a quick payoff. In line with that policy, it canceled an agreement with Intel Corporation to help develop an advanced microprocessor and also dropped plans to work with Intel on implementing the Unix operating system.

These strategies may make short-term sense. But they can set the stage for eventual disaster when these companies find themselves without the innovative products they need to compete in the global marketplace. Business writer Max Holland, author of *The Day the Machine Stopped,* comments: "Management will think you can cut back on R&D for two or three years by a half or a third. You'll only see the effects five years down the road, when you find that you're no longer competitive."

Unfortunately, too many top managements focus only inward, not outward, during the downsizing process. They look within the organization to determine what must be done, ignoring the market and other aspects of the outside environment. Result: A downsizing that can be hazardous to their long-term health.

WHERE DOWNSIZING GOES WRONG

Must downsizing inevitably damage the organization? Not necessarily. True, there is no such thing as pain-free downsizing. Nevertheless, as Robert Fierle, president of the industrial equipment maker American Precision Industries, points out, the organization can emerge from the process in better shape than before.

> It's pretty hard to sugarcoat layoffs—they're traumatic at best. But a company can be stronger for the exercise. Indirectly, U.S. business benefited from foreign competition coming in with its better quality and lower prices. We needed this kick in the can because we got a little bit lazy and fat after World War II. Restructuring is painful at the time, but in the long run the organization will be sharper and survivors of the downsizing will be happier because they'll be on a winning team instead of a losing one.

The End of Long-Term Thinking

James M. Guinan was CEO of the Caldor division of Associated Dry Goods when the parent firm of the $1.5 billion retailing chain was acquired by the May Company. The layoffs that followed, he says, resulted in the destruction of life-style and career for dozens of middle managers, particularly in the corporate office. And he observed a profound shift away from long-term thinking in the organization. He points out some examples of what this can do to the future performance of the company.

> When there was still some sense of permanence in the business world, managers could think long-term, because they knew that both they and their accomplishments would be around for many years.
> But when the predators come calling, all that goes down the drain. As a result, a subtle but devastating shift in attitude has taken place among managers. They build nothing that is for the future (except accidentally) because they know they will not be there to enjoy results way down the road. And there is no team spirit because they know the team will not exist very long. This change in priorities can wreak havoc on organizational performance.

> - A manager planning a new distribution center could once count on the center being his monument. So he would develop a center that would be effective into the future. Now that same manager would do whatever made him look good short-term—for instance, coming in well below projected cost or cutting desirable startup time—even if it meant a distribution center that was inherently inefficient and unable to meet service needs in the years ahead.
> - A financial manager might drag out payments to vendors to make her near-term balance look good, even at the expense of long-term vendor relations.
> - A human resources executive might buy short-term labor peace—even though his concessions would eventually translate into intolerable operating constraints for the company.

If this is so, then why do so many restructured companies end up with employees too distracted and demoralized to perform at their peak? Our interviews and other research indicate that some key mistakes are largely responsible for unsuccessful downsizing.

Lack of Communication—Both Up and Down

Ironically, a prime example of communication failure is provided by a major communications company. *Business Month* reported in February 1989:

> AT&T has paid a stiff price for the sloppy handling of employee communications. When the telecommunications giant was ready to launch its layoff drive in 1984, top management allowed the news to leak to the press before notifying employees and then fed out information about who was to stay and who was to go in bits and pieces. Panic set in among the rank and file, disrupting operations and delaying the company's planned growth in the computer market—a business it was heavily counting on to generate new profits. Even now, after most of the hysteria has died down, company insiders say that morale is still low and that productivity improvements have not reached hoped-for levels.

"Employee stress is a function of the amount of information that is available," observes psychological consultant John Clizbe. "The less information people have the more uptight they'll get."

He cites the trickle-down approach to communication as a major culprit. "The top people have the most information, and then it keeps getting thinner and more distorted as it filters down through the organization. As a result, employees spend an enormous amount of time standing around the hallways, the rumor mill runs rampant, and top management gets totally frustrated because productivity falls off like a brick."

American Precision Industries' Robert Fierle believes that top management makes a major mistake when it doesn't communicate about the possibilities of future downsizings. "Because management can't guarantee that restructuring won't recur, they say nothing to their employees. This is absolutely wrong, We don't give people credit for being smart. They understand what the hell the world is about. If you don't level with them, trust goes down the drain."

It's not just downward communication that is sadly ne- glected during the restructuring process. Just as bad is the short shrift given to *upward* communication. Basically, this results from management's failure to listen to its employees. A top management that insulates itself from everyone out- side the executive suite may learn too late some things that rank-and-file employees have known all along about the problems that must be fixed during a restructuring.

Rather than open up lines of communication with em- ployees throughout the organization, some senior executives will go to ridiculous extremes just to *avoid* such communica- tion. When we visited one manager at a large manufactur- ing company, the headquarters offices were in the throes of a major remodeling. The manager told us that his chairman was spending hundreds of thousands of dollars to revamp the headquarters layout so that he wouldn't have to encoun- ter any lower-level employees in going from the elevator to his office every morning.

Of course, this effort to avoid communication with em- ployees actually *did* communicate a message, since the hy- pocrisy of a supposedly cost-conscious company spending its money in this way was painfully apparent to the rest of the organization.

Another manager, for a major beauty products company, told us that his top management had always preached an open-door policy. "But if you went up to Mahogany Row with an idea or some concern you wanted to share, once you walked into an office you were a marked person. They preached open-door but didn't mean it." Nor is this an iso- lated example. A 1989 Towers Perrin survey found that one in three employees was reluctant to go over a boss's head for fear of retribution. And yet, of the companies surveyed, three out of four claimed they had open-door policies.

A major problem is that many top managements turn a deaf ear toward upward communication because they don't want to hear *bad* news. *The Wall Street Journal* cited this story of Eastman Kodak, which has gone through four restructurings in recent years:

> When a manager began tracking Fuji (a Kodak competitor), he discovered that the Japanese company had been quietly licensing Kodak technology from Kodak's patent attorneys, who didn't inform senior executives. Fuji also had a more efficient inventory system in the U.S. While Kodak warehouses stocked almost all its products, Fuji relied on overnight air shipments, which increased freight expenses but sharply reduced inventory costs and delivery times. After he presented his findings about Fuji to senior management, however, the manager, who has since left the company, says he was told never to talk about it again. "The message was, 'We don't want to hear that story,'" says the departed manager.

When managers are under pressure to succeed, they sometimes cover up the bad news. A case in point is General Electric's under-the-gun efforts to produce a new type of compressor for its refrigerators to win back lost market share. Test technicians told their bosses that the new compressors had serious defects. But that news never made it to the senior executive level. Ultimately, the cost for GE to fix or replace the thousands of compressors that were allowed to reach the market was $450 million.

Even in normal times, poor downward and upward communication can adversely affect organizational performance. During restructuring, the impact is enormously magnified. Lacking information from top management, employees fill up the vacuum with rumors—and with their jobs increasingly at risk, they keep quiet about problems to which top management should be alerted because they know that bad news is not welcome in the executive suite.

Lack of Planning

When American Management Association's Eric Rolfe Greenberg surveyed 1,084 companies about their downsizing activities in 1989, 39 percent said they were "badly" or "not well" prepared for downsizing. Yet many of these companies had already downsized or were expecting to.

It is true that emergency situations can make it impossible to thoroughly plan a downsizing (although these emergencies often result from top management's failure to watch and respond to market trends and competitors' actions). But this does not explain why companies *not* under the gun of an immediate crisis still fail to plan their downsizing adequately.

The fault, according to many of those we interviewed, lies with top management's perception of what is important. That perception is frequently focused on short-term results (reducing headcount) rather than long-term effects. Planning for the future takes a back seat to achieving instant financial returns. To any extent that planning is done, it concentrates on numbers and not on maintaining employee morale and performance.

Mindless Cutbacks

Slashing the work force without considering strategic staffing needs for now and the future can wreak havoc on the organization. Too often, the objective is simply to reduce headcount, not to thoughtfully select the heads to be eliminated. A former manager for a large telecommunications firm reported:

> Management did not go after specific players who should have been retired. The overall plan seemed to deal only with getting the numbers down and did not pay attention to the quality of the employees the company was losing. Performance in the organization has declined in the five years since the initial downsizing.

Indiscriminate downsizing is nothing new. In earlier times, Roman leaders kept their army "mean and lean" by periodically having the soldiers draw lots and then executing every tenth man (hence the term *decimation*). Today's methods may be somewhat less barbaric, but the most common approaches reflect very little strategic thinking and are more suited to cutting wood than cutting staff. Here are some of the favorites:

The Chainsaw. Climbing through the corporate tree, you saw off departments to fit a predetermined cost objective. The only problem with this popular approach is that you may saw off the tree's most vital limbs.

The Lumber Mill. Need to cut costs by 15 percent? Then just ask every department to cut its costs by that percentage. Very simple and very misguided, since not all departments and functions are of equal importance to the organization—especially after downsizing.

The Across-the-Board Chisel. Cut all salaries by 10 percent (well, maybe not *all* salaries—certainly not the CEO's). You'll be sure to reduce your work force—by encouraging your most valuable (and thus marketable) people to leave.

The Chop-Down-the-Oldest Approach. The reasoning behind this tactic is twofold: First, your older workers are your most expensive workers; and second, they're not as productive as younger workers. Besides being unlawful, this approach is also impractical. When an organization loses its older workers, it loses its memory and, along with that, its wisdom. Younger survivors will spend their time and energy reinventing the wheel—or even trying to learn the business. Very expensive. Moreover, there is simply no evidence that older workers are less productive than younger ones.

What are the results of these approaches? Mostly bad. In the cost-cutting frenzy, important functions are shortchanged. LBOs put particular pressure on companies to cut everything that does not contribute to quick returns because the most pressing need is for cash flow to pay huge debt-servicing costs.

When the overriding priority is to achieve immediate savings rather than to prepare for the future, the personnel function, for example, often takes a severe hit in the downsizing process. The sales director of a large industrial equipment firm described what happened when his company went from 22,000 to 18,000 people:

> Downsizing was pretty much across the board—every manager had a goal of 15 percent. But some groups were pruned more than others—a lot of support groups in the personnel function, such as employee counselors, were eliminated. The whole personnel area was cut by 50 percent. They weren't core people, the ones who either made or sold the product, so it was easier to get rid of them.

This approach achieved short-term economies, but it left the company without the human resources services that had become even more essential now that it was depending on fewer people to do the work.

Vital communication systems are often disrupted by indiscriminate work force reductions. Too often, internal communications staff is reduced at the very time when the need for it is greater than ever. The systems that have been put in place to inform employees about company developments may either disappear or be in such disarray that they fail to disseminate clear and accurate information. Communications staff may be kept in the dark during closed-door deliberations.

Failure to Keep Key Players

Careless downsizing leads to unwanted results. One is the loss of star performers. *Business Month* cites Atlantic Richfield Company as a typical example:

> When the oil company announced plans to cut 6,000 people from its payroll in 1985, it neglected to tell promising young managers that their jobs were safe. As a result, it lost so many stars that it tried to rehire some as consultants and had to scour the executive marketplace for replacements. One insider reports that the time wasted looking for the right

people delayed the beginning of several new projects for more than six months.

Failure to Treat People with Respect and Dignity

Generally, U.S. companies seem to be improving in the way they treat terminated employees during a downsizing. The meteoric growth of outplacement firms demonstrates that more and more downsizers are providing at least some departing employees with help in finding other jobs. Generous severance packages also help to ease the pain. Despite the trends, however, many downsizing companies don't see the need for devoting much attention to the psyches of displaced employees. Getting them out the door is the primary concern. No matter if it's done without much sensitivity because they'll be gone and soon forgotten.

Gone they will be, but not necessarily forgotten. Remaining employees will certainly remember the way their colleagues were treated—and that treatment will scarcely increase their loyalty and commitment. Talented new managers will be harder to recruit, since the reputation of a company is definitely affected by the public's memories of how it dealt with terminated employees. A classic example is Tenneco's now legendary termination of 1,200 employees in 1986. In business circles, the name Tenneco still conjures up the day that hundreds of employees discovered they were no longer employed when uniformed security guards appeared on their office floors with boxes for them to use in clearing out their desks. They were given 20 minutes to leave the building.

Similar methods were used when Atari Corporation's business collapsed in the early 1980s. Laid-off employees were escorted off the premises by security guards. Top management, rather than expressing its regret about the need for layoffs, belittled the terminated employees to those who remained. Since the survivors knew that their dismissed co-workers were no different than themselves, their belief in management's credibility went to zero.

Such horror stories surface with less frequency now. But too many companies still treat their excess employees as scrap rather than as human beings who deserve respect and dignity during a painful period in their lives. *Time* reported one example that took place late in 1989:

> Steve Snow, 36, went to work for R. J. Reynolds right after college. The son of a tobacco farmer, he worked as a Reynolds manager for 14 years. He was dismissed last month, along with 1,640 other workers, as part of the restructuring of the firm following its $25 billion buyout by Kohlberg Kravis Roberts last November. Called into the product manager's office and given the word, he recalls, "I went numb. I could not say anything for a minute. I felt like I had always done a good job and that this could not be happening to me. They decided I could not go back into the working area. I had left my dress shoes under my desk. They sent someone to get them for me."

Offering Early-Retirement Packages that Backfire

As Virginia Lord, senior vice president of Right Associates, puts it:

> Simple as the concept of offering a voluntary program sounds, it is fraught with potential hazards to both employer and employee. These include not being an attractive enough offer to thin the ranks by the approximate number desired or being so attractive as to invite far too many employees and key executives to leave, thereby decimating the company's management team, creating chaos, and resulting in higher costs rather than significant savings for the employer.

Downsizing in Waves

Downsizing companies often fail to do the job the first time. They don't want to overcut and then have to hire back employees, because this has a disastrous effect on morale. Or they miscalculate the extent of savings they will achieve through downsizing. The costs of severance pay and benefits continue even after the laid-off employees have left. This results in an immediate drop in productivity, since money is being paid to employees who cannot produce anything because they are no longer around. When a company finds that expenses have not been sufficiently reduced, it may embark on another round of layoffs.

What happens when one downsizing is followed by another—and then still another? Often, the result is serious demoralization of the remaining work force and plummeting performance. Eastman Kodak has gone through four restructurings in six years—each involving substantial layoffs. The fourth attempt to cut costs included elimination of 4,500 jobs. Employee demoralization reached the point where disgruntled Eastman Kodak workers called for the chairman's resignation in letters to the newspapers in Rochester, New York, where Kodak is located. Outside observers also criticized management for not shrinking the company in one radical restructuring rather than through repeated rounds of cutbacks.

A company cannot—and certainly should not—guarantee that the first downsizing will be the last. An unexpected downturn or other event can make further work force cuts unavoidable. But many executives believe that a company should plan to do all the downsizing it needs to do at one time. Dr. John L. Sprague is one. Now a consultant, Sprague shepherded Sprague Electric Company (now Sprague Technologies, Inc.) through a radical downsizing from 12,900 to 8,300 employees. He says: "Quite a few people say the worst thing you can do is overcut and hire back. I absolutely disagree. The worst thing you can do is undercut and then have to keep doing it. Undercutting is usually a result of poor planning."

Elizabeth Julia Cole, management and organizational development consultant for Mobil's Marketing and Refining Division, was deeply involved in the company's downsizing in the early 1980s. She says:

The layoffs were done over a period of time rather than in one fell swoop. At that time I felt it was better to do it that way than have a "Black Friday." Now I'm not so sure. Because the layoffs took place over a long time period, uncertainty overrode anything that people were doing on their jobs. They knew it was coming but they didn't know if it was going to be them or not. Their productivity was seriously impacted.

Ignoring the Impact on Survivors

Even companies that show sensitivity and concern for those who lose their jobs during a restructuring tend to forget that their remaining employees may need some help too. For example, Mobil's Cole says of her company's downsizing: "I think we did a good job in our concern and our dealing with the people who were made redundant—but what we failed to understand at the time was that we should have given as much attention to the survivors."

Too many companies, however, fail to acknowledge and address these symptoms. For some, survivor morale takes low priority at a time when restructuring and downsizing are creating intense pressures to produce with a leaner work force. Others will assume that the trauma is temporary and that their surviving employees will soon be back to normal. Actually, the wounds do not heal that quickly, and often restructuring results in permanently changed attitudes that lead to lower productivity. This is happening, for example, in the publishing industry, which has been going through constant organizational turmoil, including mergers, acquisitions, and layoffs. One publishing company executive says, "Employees are running so scared that there is a whole culture that says don't make waves—just at the time when we need innovation."

Failing to Maintain Credibility

Bunker Ramo was acquired by Allied Signal Corporation in 1981. One Bunker Ramo manager reports that the acquired company's employees were told by Allied management that there would be no changes and Bunker Ramo's corporate offices would be maintained. Within six months, the corporate offices were closed and 820 Bunker Ramo employees lost their jobs.

A sales manager in a downsized industrial equipment company said, "After the first downsizing, they told us it was over—and the next fall it happened again. Now, every October people start twitching. The company totally lost its credibility." In addition, he reported, there was loss of trust based on the belief of many managers that the painful downsizings were made necessary by top management's reckless excursions into several disastrous acquisitions unrelated to its core business.

> The business we grew up in was a nice business, a cash cow, but top management wanted more. Its attitude seemed to be, "Why don't you just stand in a corner and do your dull little jobs and crank out money so the really important guys can buy exciting new businesses that will turn us into a $5 billion corporation." But a lot of the stuff they bought turned sour and we lost money. We were overextended, so we borrowed. This made downsizing necessary. We managers felt that the very people who caused the problem were now saying to us that *we* must bear the burden for downsizing and restructuring. And it bothered us that now they were explaining their new wisdom to us just as importantly as they had previously explained how wonderful things were going to be with their exciting new acquisitions.

Credibility also erodes when top management's behavior fails to match its pronouncements. Telling managers that they must sacrifice income and jobs while awarding itself generous bonuses is scarcely calculated to stimulate trust and confidence. In 1987 General Motors laid off thousands of employees but GM executives received $157 million in stock bonuses. According to *Business Month,* Donald P. Kelly, former chairman of Beatrice Companies, "walked away from the company's LBO with a reported $20 million-plus, while some 20,000 jobs went down the tubes." And these are just two examples of recent top-management behavior that has created a credibility crisis in U.S. business.

Overlooking the "People" Factor in Mergers and Acquisitions

Merger consultant Nancy Dodd McCann observes that cash flows do not service debt, repay principal, or operate a company—people do. One wonders, then, why companies contemplating a merger or acquisition pay so little attention to evaluating the key people who will be responsible for the performance of the business.

Typically, due diligence zeroes in on the financial aspects of the merger or acquisition and neglects the people aspects. Crunching numbers takes priority over auditing the human resources of the prospective acquisition or merging partner—even though human resources are crucial to the success or failure of the restructured operation.

Similarly, many companies do not prepare adequately for the human problems that are inevitable during a merger or acquisition. "The acquiring company doesn't want to hear about people problems," says psychological consultant John Clizbe. "They've got their mind set on buying this company and they figure that after they've bought it they'll fix any problems. So they don't want to know in advance what the bad news is."

But unless management carefully plans the steps it must take to manage the transition smoothly, people will get lost amidst the heightened pressures of restructuring. Cultural clashes, stress, and uncertainty will take their toll, and people will be working against each other rather than with each other. Organization performance will slide as people are distracted from their jobs by rumors and speculation (usually evoking worst-case scenarios).

Sybil F. Stershic was marketing manager at several banks in eastern Pennsylvania, which were acquired by other bank holding companies. She describes this scenario that is all too typical:

> The lead bank's people came in and gave us what I soon realized was a lot of B.S.: We embrace you, our managements are similar, we have the same philosophies, the same corporate culture, and everything is going to be hunky-dory.
>
> Not so. Instead, there were a lot of lines set up and it became a "them" and "us" situation. They sent in a fair-haired boy from their organization to run our bank—a complete outsider who didn't know us and didn't know the community. This was resented by my bank's employees, and its customers, too. The reigning mood was paranoia, fear, and just plain panic. People weren't concentrating on their jobs— they were too busy worrying about what was going to happen to them.
>
> The worst thing was our loss of autonomy. The lead bank believed in centralized operations. We lost the authority to do things and make things happen. Before we were bought, we had an operations center located a few blocks from the main office. If you had a problem, you called Sally or Joe or George or whomever. No problem.
>
> After we were bought, that whole function was transferred to where our owner was located. All of a sudden I couldn't call on Sally or Joe or George for help. I had to call somebody out of town who I didn't know and who didn't know me.
>
> This affected our ability to serve our customers, something our employees took great pride in. When we called the centralized customer service center to get answers for our customers, their reaction was that we were spoiling them. That hurt—being told by this big organization that we were really pains in the neck for trying to get information to take care of our customers.

This is but one example of how ignoring the human problems in mergers and acquisitions can cause performance to deteriorate. Employee dissatisfaction can trigger longer lunch hours, increased absenteeism, and even more serious employee misconduct. University of Florida sociologist Richard Hollinger reported that at one family-owned company absorbed by a foreign giant, pilferage climbed dramatically because angry employees "felt abandoned by the former owners."

MAKING A DIFFICULT SITUATION WORSE

There is no way a company can downsize and restructure without at least some pain, disruption, and stress. But does it have to be done so badly? Must corporations employ mindless, destructive, ill-planned tactics when they are forced to cut people and costs? Must they treat their employees as so much ballast to be thrown over the side when the ship is sinking? Must they ignore the survivors whose trust in the organization has been shaken to the roots? Must they pocket millions in bonuses while thousands of their ex-employees are applying for unemployment checks?

No, restructuring can be done better. But it's going to take a corporate leadership that is willing to totally refocus its vision. Only then will it be able to stop shooting itself in the foot and begin restoring a healthy relationship with its managers and other employees.

A Restructuring Dictionary

align, vt: (1) to persuade employees, regardless of their own goals, to work toward an organization's goals; (2) to bend into shape one or more business units.

contingent employee, n: employee who can be quickly terminated, e.g., contract or temporary employee.

contingency planning, n: preparing to downsize.

core business, n: (1) the part of a business that management thinks it still understands; (2) that portion of a business left over after divestitures.

corporate values, n: beliefs deeply held by a CEO, e.g., employee loyalty, profit, golden parachutes.

corporate vision, n: an ideal company future, as dreamed up by the CEO (antonym: reality).

deadwood, n: employees in other departments than yours, especially older employees (synonyms: our human resources, our valued employees).

employee orientation, n: telling one's employees, especially new ones, that they'd better learn how to compete with the Japanese.

A Restructuring Dictionary (concluded)

executive offices,   n: (1) sparsely populated area of a corporate headquarters; (2) a phrase used as telephone greeting by secretaries at outplacement organizations when answering calls to job seekers.

golden parachute,   n: severance payment provided to senior executives, especially CEOs, for having lost control of their corporations; usually triggered by a change-of-control form of restructuring and a provision in the executive's contract that guarantees multiples of annual salary and other financial rewards for loss of control; variants, named for other precious metals, are provided to executives at other levels who have abetted the golden-parachute awardees in their achievements.

headcount,   n: the number of employees still on an organization's payroll, despite all efforts to reduce this number.

human resources,   n: (1) "our most important resource," as described in annual reports; (2) headcount (synonyms: employees, deadwood).

leveraged,   adj: up to one's ears in debt.

outplace,   vt: to terminate employment (synonyms: fire, lay off, both terms now obsolescent).

outplacement,   n: (1) the process of providing office space and support while an outplaced manager seeks reemployment; (2) a growth industry of the 1980s and 1990s.

plateau,   vi: to reach a sticking point in one's career, being subject thereafter only to lateral movement, if any, i.e., to locomotions rather than promotions.

rationalization,   n: (1) the act of restructuring along logical industry lines; (2) the act of trying to explain or justify in a credible manner a restructuring of an illogical nature.

redundant,   adj: an employee's condition of superfluity, which, when discovered, leads to unemployment.

restructuring,   n: (1) reorganization of ownership and/or configuration of a corporation through acquisition, buyout, divestment, downsizing, merger, public offering, recapitalization, spinoff, stock repurchase, or other means still under development; (2) America's largest domestic industry, now also globalized.

strategic planning,   n: giving thought to the next quarter's results.

synergy,   n: combining large companies in the same business (synonym: headcount reduction).

temporary employee,   n: in today's context, possibly any member of the work force.

voluntary,   adj: deriving from one's own choice, as in "voluntary early-retirement window of opportunity" (synonym: obligatory).

CHAPTER 5

CORPORATE LEADERSHIP:
CAN IT REFOCUS
ITS VISION?

When middle managers sign on, they have little control over the values of their company. They are at the mercy of the people at the top. Yes, they can run their own department and try to impose their own values, but that's quite impossible if their values are different from the CEO's. So it is up to corporate leaders to promote a set of values that fundamentally satisfy the needs and better instincts of the employees who cannot impose those values themselves. That's why we work very hard to be sure by word and deed that everyone in the organization understands that we mean to do it right. We like to say that we are an ethical, humane, and demanding corporation.

—John Hoyt Stookey, chief executive officer, Quantum Chemical Corporation

At the Sixth General Assembly of the World Future Society in 1989, Victor Pinedo, Jr., president of Corporate Transitions, Inc., made a bizarre prediction: He speculated that by the year 2010, there may be no CEOs. (It is not recorded whether this prediction was greeted by wild applause.) Pinedo went on to say that rather than our present-day, machine-like organizational structures, we might have organic structures where the direction would be provided by nonhierarchical leaders.

Pinedo's far-out forecast will have to be tested by time. It seems to ignore the need for someone at the top who can provide and consolidate a company vision. But regardless of what the future may bring, CEOs today *do* have the immense responsibility of running U.S. corporations. Individually, CEOs come in a broad variety of shapes, sizes, and styles, but collectively they represent corporate leadership in the United States. And whether they can build a new partnership with their middle managers depends largely on how they attack the trust gap that now is pervasive—provided they attack it at all.

Unfortunately, the elusive talent of corporate leadership has been overdiscussed and often underpracticed. There has been no shortage of leadership analysis. We have democratic leaders, autocratic leaders, and laissez faire leaders. People-oriented leaders and task-oriented leaders. Type X leaders and Type Y leaders. Achievement-oriented, power-oriented, and affiliation-oriented leaders. Transactional leaders and transforming leaders.

Obviously, some of the men and women described by these terms actually are leaders. But results show that many are not.

Much of the research and analysis that produced these classifications is both useful and enlightening. However, it is not this book's role to discuss corporate leadership styles. The quality of leadership comes into the picture here simply because it is pivotal in restoring trust between the company and its managers.

Why do we say that corporate leadership is underpracticed? For one thing, too many corporate chieftains fail to *apply* the leadership values that they *preach*. Result: distrust. As management authority Richard E. Byrd puts it:

> The biggest pitfall for a corporate leader is that he or she will be inconsistent in applying values. The credibility gap that

may result can lead to accusations of hypocrisy, cynicism, and malaise on the part of employees. Moreover, employees may end up taking nothing management says at face value.

And yet, as John Hoyt Stookey contends in the paragraph that opened this chapter, a primary job of top management is to shape the values of the organization. How well are corporate leaders doing that?

If you ask the thousands of alienated managers in this country, the answer is *not very*. Values are meaningful only if they become part of the day-to-day work beliefs of corporate leaders. Only then will managers and other employees equate *espoused* company values with *actual* company values.

In too many companies today, proclaimed values clash with practiced values. Executives may mouth all the right phrases. They might talk about pushing decision making downward, about wanting better quality, about the importance of ethical behavior. They may even send their people to seminars and distribute high-sounding credos for them to sign. And yet all too often those same executives will then demonstrate very clearly that they don't really mean it. They'll order managers to ship a defective product to the customer, saying, "It's not perfect, but we've got to get it out the door." Or they'll overrule managers' decisions without even giving them a hearing. Meanwhile, people down the line are watching very closely to find out whether the company means what it says or whether company policy is just words. In many cases they don't have to watch that closely, because the disparities are all too obvious.

At the other extreme, heads of some of our most successful business organizations clearly demonstrate their belief in their human resources as the wellspring of their success by continuing to invest heavily in and remaining committed to their people—their team. IBM, for example, has maintained a full-employment policy through more than 60 years, including the long, dark era of the Great Depression. The company remains committed to the firmly held conviction of its founder, Thomas J. Watson, Sr., who believed that long-term corporate success was based on unswerving values—one of them being the worth of the individual. Even though IBM has found some downsizing to be unavoidable, it has utilized early-retirement incentives and redeployment rather than layoffs. Delta Airlines and Federal Express are two other companies with no-layoff policies.

Closing today's trust gap requires that corporate leaders commit themselves to similar philosophical values. Unless they make those commitments, no attempt to change the corporate culture will make the slightest difference. In fact, empty buzzwords and quick-fix programs will only leave managers more cynical than before.

SHIFTING THE COMMITMENTS

Some U.S. companies are making a genuine effort to close the trust gap. Some are ignoring it and focusing on other priorities. Still others are acknowledging the problem but hoping it will go away all by itself (it won't).

A number of key characteristics of corporate leadership contribute to either widening the trust gap or closing it. They might be called trust busters and trust enhancers.

Trust Busters	*Trust Enhancers*
• Leaders give priority to shareholders over all other corporate constituencies.	• Leaders balance the needs of all constituencies: customers, employees, owners, suppliers, communities.
• Leaders sacrifice long-term needs to short-term advantages.	• Leaders balance short-term needs with the long-term health of the company.
• Leaders rely on buzzwords and quick fixes to address serious corporate problems.	• Leaders make a strong commitment to genuine and continuous change.

- Leaders use manipulation and hypocritical pronouncements to keep the troops in line.
- Leaders play the power role of isolated, luxury-loving feudal lords.

- Leaders are technocrats who understand only methodology and quantification.

- Leaders practice honest communication and support what they say with action.
- Leaders play the service role of getting close to customers and supporting employees.
- Leaders understand the need to establish a cohesive corporate culture that maximizes human potential.

SHAREHOLDERS AND SHORT-TERM MANAGEMENT

The 1980s saw a relentless focus on deal making and short-term financial management. American management acted as if there were no tomorrow—their attitude seemed to be that the party would soon be over, so cash in while you can. Long-term concerns—among them the crucial problem of establishing a healthier relationship between companies and their managers—took a backseat. The damage has been extensive. Managers—middle managers in particular—have been treated as pawns in the takeover and merger games that have dominated the past decade. Repairing the damage will require a major shift in focus by corporate leaders who, for the most part, have been listening only to their shareholders.

The word *shareholder* 20 years ago may have conjured up the image of a little old lady in Dubuque with two shares of General Electric. But a funny thing happened on the way to the 1980s. All the little old ladies and other individual shareholders steadily dwindled as a percentage of U.S. investors. In 1965 individual shareholders represented 84 percent of all shareholders—by 1980 they were down to 70 percent, and as we went into the 1990s the figure was barely more than 50 percent.

The little old ladies have been replaced by huge institutional investors—pension funds, mutual funds, and money managers. By the end of 1989, institutions owned 60 percent of the stock of companies on the Standard & Poor's 500 list.

Because shareholders are "owners," many believe that their interests should take precedence over everyone else. But institutional investors don't necessarily think of themselves as "owners," if ownership means having a vested interest in the long-term health of the company. Institutional investors generally have shown only a transient interest in the companies in which they have bought stock. Andrew C. Sigler, chairman and CEO of Champion International Corporation, recalls that while attending meetings of his own company's pension committee he never once heard any committee members mention the names of the companies they held. Instead, he said, "It was all what percentile, what quartile, how did they do last month."

Pension funds and other institutional investors also abdicate their ownership role when they invest large amounts of their portfolios in leveraged-buyout funds such as those of Kohlberg Kravis Roberts & Company. The investors have no direct control over what is done with their money. Instead, they become passive bystanders, while managers of the LBO funds call the shots. The investors' role is so small, says James George, investment manager of the $9 billion Oregon Public Employees' Retirement System, that he often learns of an investment planned by Kohlberg Kravis when he picks up a newspaper, even though he has a $50 million investment in their fund.

When institutional investors collaborate with LBO funds, the focus is inevitably on the "deal" rather than on the company involved. Until the end of the 1980s, institutional investors seldom objected to takeover attempts—in fact they usually backed them with enthusiasm since threat of a takeover meant a terrific short-term boost for their investments. But as Peter Drucker wrote late in 1989:

> The raiders are surely right to assert that a company must be run for performance rather than for the benefit of its management. They are, however, surely wrong in defining "performance" as nothing but immediate, short-term gains for shareholders. This subordinates all other constituencies—above all, managerial and professional employees—to the immediate gratification of people whose only interest in the business is short-term payoffs.

Drucker zeros in on a serious problem that involves basic corporate and social values: allowing one corporate constituency to take overwhelming priority over all others. Doing so produces a potentially disastrous imbalance among these constituencies, which include not only the owners but employees, customers, creditors, suppliers, and the communities in which the company operates. Indeed, as environmental concerns continue to increase, the general public—and the planet itself—can legitimately be thought of as constituencies of the corporation. But the more equitable balance of constituencies in the past has been replaced by one overriding concern: enhancing the wealth of shareholders.

The Japanese chairman of a U.S. company's subsidiary in Japan told Tom Horton: "It used to be said that U.S. companies had forgotten their customers. Today, many U.S. companies have also forgotten their employees."

Plenty of U.S. employees would agree. One disillusioned 20-year worker told *Business Week:* "We used to be a community—employees, shareholders, lots of groups ... Now it's clear there is only one important group—the shareholders."

Some corporate leaders themselves are acutely aware of the problem. "A U.S. public company is controlled in many ways by the quarterly reports it has to produce for its share-holders," says Kenneth Draeger, president and chief operating officer (COO) of Agfa Corporation. "That has a tendency to produce a short-term attitude about your business."

Champion's Andrew C. Sigler puts it even more strongly: "The only pressure I have on me is short-term pressure. I announce that we're going to spend half a billion dollars at Courtland, Alabama, with a hell of a payout from redoing a mill, and my stock goes down two points."

A similar example involves the Martin Marietta Corporation. When the company announced plans to boost its R&D spending, Wall Street money managers reacted by dumping their shares because of the possible effect on short-term earnings. The company's stock skidded by six points.

There are those who believe that what is good for shareholders is good for all the other corporate constituencies, such as employees and customers. Quantum's CEO John Hoyt Stookey disagrees sharply. He paints a gloomy picture of what happens to managers when corporations are stripped of cash on behalf of shareholders:

> The shareholders extract the maximum current value from the enterprise. That inevitably tends to stop the ship dead in the water. Capital expenditures go down to a maintenance level and a lot of things get cut back. People lose their jobs and for those who remain there is a significant hiatus in the natural, normal growth expectations of their careers. *They get put on hold in the same way that the enterprise gets put on hold.* And this is all in the interest of maximum cash to one side of the equation. Therefore, I believe that to a certain degree some of the cash that gets taken out doesn't rightfully belong to the shareholder because he has cashed in on the future that has been promised to those managers, who don't share in the spoils.

Stookey has expressed a crucial concept. He is not saying that shareholders have no rights *but that their rights must not be allowed to infringe on the equally important rights of other stakeholders in the organization, particularly employees.* Needless to say, this is not a popular concept on Wall Street.

The trust gap between managers and their employers will never be closed by short-term thinking. Building a new partnership is a lengthy process—not something that can be accomplished overnight. NCR Chairman and CEO Charles E. Exley, Jr., talks about long-term management in terms of "building capability." The quality of the people in management, he says, is key to carrying out a company's long-term mission.

The good news is that taking this approach may be easier for corporate leaders to do in the future. As the 1990s began, the threat of corporate takeovers seemed to be decreasing. Investors scared off by the fate of several heavily leveraged takeovers and the collapse of Drexel Burnham Lambert lost their enthusiasm for the junk bonds that fueled the takeover surge. Some observers believe that corporate CEOs may now be less distracted by the problem of beating raiders away from their doors and can get back to the business of running their companies.

Others think it is too early to declare the demise of corporate raiding and restructuring. Robert D. Ferris, executive vice president of Doremus Public Relations, commented that Federal Reserve Board Chairman Alan Greenspan's 1989 pronouncement that "the end of the corporate restructuring of this nation is at hand," reminded some observers of Neville Chamberlain's "peace in our time" speech back in 1938. Even though junk bonds are in some disrepute, raiding may take other, more sophisticated forms. Wall Street investment bankers and lawyers would be loath to give up the enormous fees that pour into their coffers from takeovers and mergers (in the $14 billion merger of Time, Inc., and Warner Communications, Inc., in 1989, six investment firms pocketed $125 million in fees). Blackstone Group Chairman Peter G. Peterson was quoted as saying that corporate raiding will continue because "there's so much money to be made in fees that these Wall Street geniuses are going to find ways to do it."

There are some who would be loath to see corporate raiding disappear because they credit the pressure of take-over threats with keeping management on its toes and forcing it to "get rid of the flab." However, many of the changes made by companies under the gun of takeover threats, such as dumping employees indiscriminately and cutting capital and R&D investment, are not healthy for the long-term future of the concern.

Moreover, even without corporate raiding there would still be intense pressures on management to perform. These pressures will come from relentless global competition. Surprisingly, they may also come from the very institutional investors that concentrated only on short-term returns during the 1980s. For as the new decade opened, some pension funds seemed to be shifting away from their short-term mentality. As Peter Drucker put it, "They are beginning to think through their obligation to a business as a going concern." If true, this could have a salutary effect for top managers who wish to achieve a more rational balance between short-term and long-term objectives.

But this balance cannot be achieved unless corporate leaders take the initiative in building cultures that not only inspire trust and commitment from managers, but also give them a major role in helping to make their organizations strong enough to meet the unprecedented challenges of the 1990s. Among the things they must do are to eliminate top-management isolation, communicate and *act* upon strong corporate values, and make a genuine, long-term commitment to *real* change in the organization.

ISOLATIONISM: TOP-MANAGEMENT STYLE

"No man is an island," wrote John Donne in the 17th century. But some 20th century CEOs seem to have forgotten that. They are often totally isolated from the people in their organizations beyond a few top managers. This only serves to widen the trust gap.

It's not that corporate leaders aren't busy. A 1990 *Fortune* poll of 206 CEOs showed they work an average of 61 hours a week. Dealing with the constant demands on their time is not easy. (Management has been described as a series of interruptions interrupted by interruptions.) A CEO's job is further complicated by the increasing pressures of severe global competition, threats of hostile takeovers, technological revolutions, unpredictable shifts in economic conditions, constantly changing regulations, and geopolitical surprises.

Lack of time may be one contributing factor to why so many corporate leaders have virtually isolated themselves from the rest of the organization—to the extent that *they don't even know that there is a tremendous amount of distrust and cynicism among their own managers*. But there are other, darker explanations. Some CEOs have isolated themselves through apparently deliberate choice. They don't want to know what their employees are thinking, especially if it's negative. Nobody likes criticism—and CEOs probably like it less than the rest of the population. (In contrast, however, the best CEOs *welcome and even seek out* criticism.)

Some CEOs have isolated themselves from employees through their bloated incomes and fantasy-world perks. It's difficult for a $40,000-a-year middle manager to relate to a CEO who makes 100 times that and indulges in million-dollar apartments, game hunts in India, and dove shoots in Mexico—especially when that middle manager is being exhorted to cut costs to the bone. (European and Japanese CEOs seldom earn more than 15 times the lowest-paid employee's wages.)

The trust gap yawns even wider when employees realize that much of this enormous compensation is not closely linked to performance. Ostensibly, top executives who receive stock options gain only when the shareholder gains.

But in a study of 214 large U.S. companies, Professor Graef S. Crystal of Berkeley's Haas School of Business found almost no correlation between executive option gain and shareholder price appreciation. And a study of the relationship between CEO pay and performance in 1,000 companies by Harvard Professor Michael Jensen and University of Rochester Professor Kevin Murphy found that only about 3 percent of a CEO's total cash compensation is actually at risk every year.

Most employees have no problem with the *concept* of pay differentials based on corporate rank. It's the constantly escalating *size* of the differential that has them muttering. A study by the polling firm, Sirota Alper & Pfau, shows that of a random sample of 350 employees, two thirds thought CEOs got too big a share. But then, how many CEOs have asked their employees what they think of executive salaries? And how many seem to care?

Another factor contributing to the isolation of top management from its employees is the failure in downward communication. The CEO may communicate strategies and missions to the senior executives just below him—but then they get no further. Says Peter Gelfond, partner and director of employee survey programs at the Hay Group:

> I recently made presentations to three Fortune 100 companies based on the results of their corporate wide employee survey programs. I had to tell them that their biggest problem is what I call a "hierarchy gap." While the senior executives have positive attitudes toward the organization, the next level of management below them doesn't. That's because senior executives are isolating themselves from middle managers. As a result, middle managers are beginning to see the organization the same way that hourly employees see it— which is not as favorably as senior management. In higher performing companies, our data show very little gap between senior management's attitudes about the organization and the attitudes of the next level of management.

Tom Wheeler, CEO of Massachusetts Mutual Life Insurance Company, makes a similar point:

> We CEOs spend a lot of time developing our strategies. But what often happens is that we build up this huge book of strategies and then immediately put it on the shelf and say, "Okay, whew, we're done with that, now we can move on and get down to business."

This is confirmed by the *Fortune* poll of CEOs, which asked them how large U.S. companies should better manage their managers. Only 10 percent mentioned communicating a corporate mission, and only 5 percent mentioned encouraging better communication in general. Yet in our interviews with middle managers, the most *frequently* mentioned top management fault was poor communication.

Leaders of high-performing companies often see their relationship with employees in an unusual way. Their attitude is: *I work for my employees—I am here as a resource for them, to give them a sense of direction, a sense of mission.* Unfortunately, there is an acute shortage of such leaders, which is one reason we have a trust gap that rivals the Grand Canyon. Psychological consultant John Clizbe describes an American Management Association course for presidents in which the participants were asked to list the groups they worked for. "They listed stockholders, boards of directors, the community, and a million other groups, but only two mentioned their employees," says Clizbe.

A trust gap is not the only unfortunate result of top-management isolationism. Another result of walling themselves off from the rest of the organization is that CEOs cut themselves off from valuable information that could help them run the business better. "These companies are dysfunctional," says polling executive David Sirota. "Top management isn't hearing what it needs to hear about markets, competitors, problems, and opportunities."

What is the answer to top-management isolationism? It can best be given by examples of executives who refuse to practice it. Instead, they do as much as they can to *break down* the barriers between themselves and their employees. Tom Wheeler, whom we just quoted, is one example. When he took over as CEO of Mass Mutual in 1988, he—along with his top management group—had already worked hard to develop a strategic vision for the company. One of his early actions as CEO was to communicate this vision to the whole organization:

> We held five separate meetings among our associates with about 800 at each meeting. I personally explained the overall vision of the company and tried to give them a feeling for what our driving force was and what the businesses were all about. These meetings were followed by divisional meetings, and then departmental meetings, to discuss how the vision related to each area. We had similar meetings with our field personnel—in fact, we took a road show out and covered the whole country until we had talked to about 5,000 field-force people. We also published a brochure on corporate strategy and on what we believed was the compact between the company and our associates.

Another example of the nonisolationist leader is Reuben Mark, CEO of Colgate-Palmolive. Claudia H. Deutsch describes in the *New York Times* how, from the day he became chief executive, he spent a huge amount of time breakfasting and lunching with employees around the world, asking them about their problems and where he could help. He also bombarded the company subsidiaries with videotapes, some describing promising new technologies and products, others spelling out corporate problems.

Tom Nies is CEO and president of Cincom Systems, Inc., the world's largest privately held computer software company with more than 1,600 employees. He is also the antithesis of the isolationist top manager. In a 1989 interview with *Industry Week,* he made a telling observation: "The senior executive of an organization must be the servant of those who are serving his customers and his other people." He translates this philosophy into action by extensive *per-*

sonal communication with Cincom employees. "The CEO has to see and be seen by his employees," he says. "You can't run this business by the numbers and simply look at rating sheets. An active, physical presence is essential."

Like most successful leaders these CEOs want to know what's *really happening*. Rather than isolating themselves from reality, they want to deal with it directly. They seek out *bad* news even more relentlessly than *good* news so that they can nip problems in the bud. Too often, the information that reaches the top is colored or filtered, and the successful chief executive is well aware of this. Countless corporate disasters can be traced to the fact that vital information did not reach the top.

These leaders also perceive sharply the purpose of their organizations and share their perceptions with their employees. While their visions for the future of their companies are sometimes called dreams, they are not that. Instead, they are clearly etched images of future possibilities rooted deeply in the realities of today.

Successful leaders also create a strategic focus. One of their key roles is to pull their companies into the future. Aware of changes in customer demand, alert to new technological developments, they constantly look for ways to reach out in new directions—to guide and transform their organizations so that they will be as prepared for tomorrow as they are for today.

If the company's focus is to be changed dramatically, the change must be clearly articulated and the new vision must be sold to managers and employees at all levels. For if it is to work, this vision must be accepted throughout the company by all who must implement it. If the vision is too ambitious it will fail, and the CEO will lose credibility. If it is not bold *enough,* nobody will catch fire. Most important, no matter how good the vision, it will never be achieved if it is not communicated to everyone in the organization. That is why there must be an end to executive isolationism.

RESTORING ETHICAL VALUES

The 1980s may go down in business history as the Decade of the Deal or the Greed Decade, but certainly not as the Ethical Decade. Savings and loan debacles, insider trading scandals, and takeover deals with greed and ego as seemingly the only motivators have all been exhaustively chronicled by the media. In March 1990 the second- and third-place books on the *New York Times* best-seller list were *Liar's Poker,* about greedy goings-on at Salomon Brothers investment bank, and *Barbarians at the Gate,* an unflattering account of the takeover struggle for RJR Nabisco, Inc.

The ethics debacle affects both Wall Street and corporate America. Henry B. Schacht, CEO of Cummins Engine Company, says, "We're mirrors of each other," maintaining that Wall Street deal makers served the requirements that were laid down to them by their corporate clients.

Some observers claim that the breakdown in business ethics has been blown up out of all proportion. This is hard to accept if one simply reads the daily press. For example, the *New York Times* issues of September 15 and 16, 1989, carried the following headlines:

EX-ASHLAND CHIEF PLEADS GUILTY

DRUG EXECUTIVE IS SENTENCED

JAIL TERM FOR EX-OFFICER OF UNISYS

U.S. REGULATORS SUE OWNERS IN BIG SAVINGS UNIT FAILURE

In the same month, the *Wall Street Journal's* lead story for September 11 was:

COOKING THE BOOKS: HOW PRESSURE TO RAISE SALES LED MINISCRIBE TO FALSIFY NUMBERS

In November of that year, the former president of Beech-Nut Nutrition Corporation admitted that he had knowingly sold artificially flavored sugar water to consumers who believed they were buying pure apple juice for their babies.

On February 27, 1990, Northrop Corporation pleaded guilty to 34 counts of falsely certifying that the parts for the Marine Corps' Harrier jet and the Air Force's Cruise missile had been properly tested. As part of the plea bargain, the United States agreed to drop its investigations of alleged Northrop improprieties related to the MX missile and the B-2 Stealth bomber.

And this is just a sparse sampling. Small wonder that a 1989 Louis Harris poll conducted for *Business Week* found that the American public has deep misgivings about business ethics. Another Harris poll in the same year, of 1,500 white-collar employees, showed that while 87 percent thought it very important for management to be honest, upright, and ethical, *only 39 percent believed that it was.*

The moral tone of any organization is inevitably set by its chief's actions, not by a company's written code of ethics, which is frequently filed away and forgotten. If, in the executive office, a corner is cut here, a decision shaded there, it tells managers two things: First, the company does not expect you to adhere to a code of ethics in doing your job (after all *I* don't!) and second, don't depend on the company to treat you ethically as an employee. Thus the trust gap opens still another troubling notch.

This was perfectly illustrated by ITT in the days of the "Geneen Machine." When Harold Geneen headed the company, according to the *New York Times:*

> ITT managers quickly learned to do whatever was expedient to avoid the chairman's wrath. "Geneen gave people the sense that their entire careers depended on how well they did with each project," recalled Howard J. Aibel, ITT's general counsel and a 25-year company veteran. "So people would proceed without caring much about how what they did affected ITT's reputation."

How practical is it to be ethical in corporate behavior? Some cynics will cite Leo Durocher's remark: "Nice guys finish last." In business, as in life, that's not necessarily true. Sometimes, the bad guys finish last. There are many corporate leaders who manage to achieve great success while at the same time acting with scrupulous integrity. Marvin Bower once observed that the company with high principles generates greater drive and effectiveness because its employees know "they can do the *right* thing decisively and with confidence."

But, in many companies, managers discover that trying to do the right thing can be hazardous to their career health. A 1989 survey by two Columbia University business school professors brought out some troubling facts. Forty percent of 1,070 alumni from the classes of 1953 through 1987 said they had been implicitly or explicitly rewarded for taking some action they considered to be ethically questionable, while only 20 percent were rewarded for refusing to do something ethically wrong. And 31 percent of those who did refuse to take some ethically doubtful action said that they had actually been penalized. One marketing manager recommended scrapping a new product that could contain toxins. He was ordered to proceed, and then got his pink slip three months later.

Although some observers believe that CEOs tend to be less burdened with scruples and hence more inclined to let the ends justify the means, corporate leaders as a group are probably no less ethical than society in general. But people who wield enormous power—whether in business or government—have an even greater duty to be more circumspect in their behavior than those whose actions affect few people besides themselves. Tom Horton made this point in his book *What Works for Me:*

> Underlying the skills and capabilities of successful chief executives is the essential quality of integrity. Without integrity, there can be no trust. Leadership is based on trust, and effective management is fueled by it.

Integrity implies a wholeness, a completeness, an integration of values. Yet one person's values are not those of another. Through reflection a manager can develop an understanding of his or her own values; by actions and words, they can be understood by others. This is crucially important, for just as managers dislike surprises, so do the people who work for and with them.

Personal integrity also implies a firm adherence to a system of ethics, a set of guiding beliefs that are gradually forged by each individual and repeatedly tested in the crucible of one's life. . . . Integrity does *not* reside in the mouthing of pompous platitudes. Nor does it imply rigidity. Indeed, successful chief executives exercise great flexibility in their thoughts and actions, yet draw a clear line at ethical limits beyond which they will not go. . . . It is only through the actual practice of integrity that the valuable asset of trust can be forged and maintained.

AN IMPERATIVE FOR
CORPORATE LEADERSHIP

The trust gap between corporate leaders and their managers confronts U.S. business with a problem that cuts to the core of its ability to compete. When managers who are charged with carrying out the CEO's strategic vision either don't know what that vision is or don't believe in it, the organization will have no more direction than a rudderless ship. All efforts to implement company strategies will be frustrated, simply because top executives and managers have totally different perspectives.

Bringing these perspectives closer together will require more than quick-fix programs and panaceas. Before anything can happen, top management must first acknowledge—at least to itself—that it is part of the problem. Only then will it be able to attack the trust gap at all. This cannot be just a program, but must be an ongoing commitment, a new way of business life—not just exhorting the troops to put out, but showing them why they should do it. Not just filling the air with buzzwords, but actually living them. ("If I hear the phrase 'empowering employees' from our CEO one more time, I may quit," said one middle manager. "Nothing's really changed around here, it's just a pretty phrase.")

With a genuine desire to close the trust gap, corporate leaders can initiate the actions that are critically needed to reduce the trauma of downsizing and restructuring, help managers adapt to new and often unfamiliar roles, and build a new partnership based on the realities of today's world.

CHAPTER 6

CURING THE DOWNSIZING
BLUES: GUIDELINES
FOR ACTION

When I lost my job, the company didn't treat me like a suspicious character with my nose pressed against the glass door saying, gee, remember me, while they were calling the security guard and saying don't let this guy in the building. Instead, during the whole process I was treated like a human being, like someone with dignity who had been a contributor to the company and was respected. Believe me, I was still hurting inside, but the way they handled it helped to ease the pain.

    —A middle manager remembering when he learned he no longer had a job

No matter how well a restructuring is managed, some people are going to be hurt through loss of job, loss of advancement opportunities, or loss of potential compensation increases—not to mention loss of self-esteem or even identity. Any change causes stress and anxiety. However, the negative effects of restructuring on the people involved can be minimized—and rather than damaging a company's performance, restructuring *can* produce a healthy improvement in the company's ability to compete and thrive. To achieve this happy result, however, requires:

- Careful planning with a long-term viewpoint.
- Thorough, open, and honest communication throughout the organization.

- Humane and caring treatment of terminated employees.
- Sensitive dealing with the problems of survivors to help them maintain morale, performance, and commitment.

TAKE TIME TO PLAN

The amount of time companies devote to planning their downsizing varies sharply from one situation to another. In hostile takeovers, there is often little time for planning the strategic and human aspects of the restructuring. Even with friendly takeovers, planning may be minimal, since attention is focused on shareholders' interests. When a company starts restructuring on its own initiative, it would seem to have more time to plan, yet it is often harried—and hurried—by intense pressure from its competition.

These and other factors contribute to the failure of most companies to plan their restructurings adequately. A hastily conceived downsizing is almost always a poorly executed one that creates widespread lack of confidence among employees. On the other hand, a downsizing that follows a carefully developed, thoroughly communicated plan can have far more positive results. Employees are more likely to take pride in the new, lean organization and to respect management for recognizing current realities and acting on them.

To be done well, downsizing requires careful analysis, consultative decision making, and precisely targeted actions. An analogy is useful: When surgery is indicated, the doctor needs to consider the long-term health of the patient before starting to cut. Even the best surgeon requires a strong support staff, each of whom understands what is being operated upon and why. And a scalpel is more appropriate in the operating room than a meat axe.

Planning a downsizing must start not with preparing the actual "surgery" but with reviewing the long-range strategies of the organization. This is the time to focus on the organization's *essential* goals and to decide what tasks *must* be performed to achieve them. By determining exactly what needs to be done, management will be better able to pinpoint the people needed to do it.

The next step is to look for areas of overlapping responsibility and functions that might be consolidated effectively. An organization may have become highly decentralized during periods of growth, so that some functions are duplicated at different locations. Whenever there's a crunch, such functions can be centralized. This will result in a need for fewer people and can help to streamline the organization just when fast—but informed—decisions are vital. Management should also consider which functions might be maintained by a small number of key people, at least over the short term.

With this analysis, a company can avoid indiscriminate across-the-board work force reductions that often cut out critical functions and people and leave the organization weaker just when it needs to be stronger. In fact, it may even be beneficial to *expand* some parts of the organization while severely cutting others.

Planning Ahead: How Du Pont Downsized

During the 1980s, Du Pont embarked on a major restructuring that eventually included a work force reduction of 14,000 employees. However, the first planning sessions did not touch upon downsizing at all, according to John P. McAndrews, retired group vice president of Du Pont Automotive Products. Instead, the planners tried to define what kind of a company Du Pont was and what it wanted to achieve in the future. Their conclusions: As a research-based company, it wanted to maintain and improve its research capabilities. As a manufacturing company, it wanted to strengthen its production efficiency with capital investment in better equipment. As a customer-driven company, it wanted to widen market interfaces so it could be closer to its customers.

To these goals, Du Pont added another: to become a more flexible, faster-moving organization capable of meeting and beating worldwide competition. This goal, the company realized, required a substantial downsizing to eliminate the bureaucratic layers and redundancies that had developed over the years in Du Pont as it had in so many other U.S. companies.

Only after establishing these goals and strategies did Du Pont planners address the actual process of downsizing—once they were able to choose the right actions to reflect their long-range objectives. (However, despite its careful planning, Du Pont was surprised by the number of employees who accepted its early retirement option—and it lost some employees it wanted to keep.)

Bringing People Experts Front and Center

In too many companies that we examined, top management failed to fully utilize the input of its human resources department in planning its downsizing. That this failure is widespread has been borne out by other sources. For example, a 1989 survey jointly sponsored by the American Society of Personnel Administration and Commerce Clearing House showed that in most corporate restructurings, human resources executives are not involved early enough to make a difference. It may be no coincidence that in many of these realignments poor employee morale and loss of key personnel were major problems. Almost 70 percent of the respondent companies experienced a deterioration of employee morale and a drop in loyalty to the company. University of Texas Professor David A. Gray believes this often happened because human resources executives were brought into the restructuring process too late, and thus were forced to react to what had already been done rather than being able to participate in planning a smooth transition. Among the things they might have done if they had been consulted earlier would be to establish an effective communication program, ease the exits of departing employees, and develop survivor programs to retain key employees.

Bringing the human resources department in early is absolutely essential, believes John Sprague, former CEO of Sprague Electric Company and currently president of John L. Sprague Associates, a Lexington, Massachusetts–based consulting firm. He describes the close consultative relationship he had with his human resources head while Sprague's downsizing was being planned:

> The resource head's office was right next to mine and we were in constant contact during the planning phase. With his input, we worked out exactly what we were going to do before we made any announcement. We knew by name those individuals who would be let go and we knew those who would be asked to stay on for an interim period. The severance arrangements were completely worked out. We ended up with a complete planning manual for the downsizing operation.

Another admirable example of downsizing planning is Central Soya, a leading agribusiness company based in Fort Wayne, Indiana, which operates more than 65 plants and facilities worldwide. After selling its food-processing businesses in 1985, the company substantially downsized its corporate office. Mack E. Wootton, a Central Soya vice president, reported that planning for this reduction included these elements:

- Each division and department went through a zero-based staffing exercise and determined the positions within each unit that should be retained.
- A formal Fort Wayne Reduction Program was developed to identify the continuing organizational structure, the jobs to be eliminated, and the people affected.
- To ensure objectivity, a reduction review committee was established to which each division and department presented its plan.
- A communication plan was developed so that employees would know how the downsizing process would work.

- Outside outplacement services in the form of group assistance to nonexempts and individual assistance to exempt employees were included in the plan.

Planning a Merger

Mergers add still another dimension to the required planning process. When two companies combine, an additional set of potential problems must be anticipated. Cultural clashes, the victor-vanquished syndrome, and personnel redundancies can all contribute to a climate of anxiety and hostility—and rob the merger of its expected benefits. Nor will these benefits flow from top-management pronouncements on the virtues of synergy. If managers have lost confidence in their leaders, exhortations for cooperation and teamwork may fall on deaf, if not cynical, ears.

Strategic planning requires that top management— in consultation with other levels of management—think through the human implications of a merger as well as its financial and business aspects.

M. E. Cooper, Chevron's general manager of purchasing, is a veteran of the 1984 Gulf-Chevron merger, which in dollar terms was the largest U.S. corporation merger to that date. Cooper believes that before a merger is consummated management must try every way possible to allow time for careful study and review. He explained:

> It shouldn't be a precipitous overnight situation where you have to complete the merger by some date next month. Time should be taken to form joint planning teams with representatives from both companies carefully selected for their abilities—not just a few designated dummies there for cosmetic reasons. During our own premerger planning we had about 37 different study teams comprised of both Chevron and Gulf people, who looked at every aspect of the business. These teams were democratically composed, not dominated by Chevron, even though Chevron was the acquiring company. As a result of the work done by these teams, the merger was

implemented with the benefit of considerable thought and care. Chevron handled the merger in a highly professional and humanitarian way, making sure everything would mesh together with a minimum of friction.

Because the Federal Trade Commission mandated a "hold separate" period before their contemplated merger could take place, Gulf and Chevron had more time than most companies for planning. But often it's not a question of time, it's a question of what is done with the time. Rather than devoting themselves exclusively to crunching numbers, the planners must pay more attention to the human problems involved in mergers and takeovers. This is not a fuzzy prescription for the milk of human kindness, but an imperative bearing directly on the health of the organization's future bottom line.

Cooper is convinced that fairness by the acquiring company pays off not only in higher morale after the merger but in a better-performing work force. Following the merger, he visited a Chevron refinery and met with eight materials managers:

> I looked around the room and realized that four managers were formerly Gulf and four were originally Chevron. It wasn't by design, it just happened, but it clearly demonstrated to me the equitable way in which employees were selected to remain with the merged company. The best of both companies were chosen, and that happened all the way down the line. The result was that we had the top performers we needed to make the merger successful.

Merger consultant Nancy Dodd McCann believes that companies should make more use of their human resources staff in analyzing and planning a merger. Too many companies, she maintains, put their human resources people to work as "handholders" *after* the merger has been completed, rather than gaining their input *before* the merger. "They must be used at the front end of the merger, rather than being brought in at the back end to mop up during the assimilation process," she says.

Unfortunately, when merging companies do consider people-related issues at all, they usually focus on visible costs such as benefits and compensation, while ignoring potential hidden costs such as sinking productivity, culture shock, and low morale. McCann believes these costs can be minimized or eliminated by thorough analysis and planning before the merger.

COMMUNICATE, COMMUNICATE, AND COMMUNICATE

What will happen to me? What's going to happen to my position? To my people? Promotions or demotions? More responsibility or less responsibility? Relocations or layoffs? What's going on here, anyway?

Questions like these keep spinning through the minds of employees involved in restructuring. Change involves a period of anxiety and uncertainty—and if there's an information vacuum, any incident will be blown up out of all proportion and no one will feel safe.

This potentially poisonous climate can be countered only by direct and frequent communications. While the names of those who must be terminated cannot be revealed before decisions are final and the people involved have been privately notified, all other important matters should be communicated fully. And if management *can't* tell its people who will be affected, then it can at least tell them that it can't tell them. Even if it's bad news, people prefer some kind of communication to no communication at all. Everyone will get through this difficult time more easily if management conveys corporate realities clearly and *honestly* throughout the organization.

All communication channels should be utilized: company newsletters, personal letters, formal meetings, and informal rap sessions. But it's not enough to rely entirely on normal, established communication channels. In addition, management should set up special communication facilities to help employees prepare for the transition, give them a chance to air their fears and hopes, and provide them with counseling and social support.

Norbert J. Kubilus, vice president of Optimal Solutions, Inc., who has been involved in downsizings at several high-tech firms, says his experience has convinced him that the usual approach of "Go talk to your manager" doesn't work. For one thing, the employee's manager may not be there anymore, may know no more than the employee does, or may be too bent out of shape to listen to someone else's problems. Says Kubilus: "The company must establish a focal point to which people can go for help, information, and clarification, preferably an independent group set up for that purpose."

Kubilus also believes that management should not rely on verbal communication alone—written communication is also important. Too often, companies convey information verbally, only to have an employee go home and say to his or her spouse, "Look, they told us about a big change, and I think they said this or that. I'm not sure, and I don't know what's going to happen." Result: confusion and anxiety. The employee should be able to bring home a piece of paper that gives details on what the options are.

If management doesn't have certain information, says Kubilus, it should tell employees when the information will be available. That can help to reduce speculation and rumor. (But if management promises to release information by a certain date, it should be sure to do it.)

Undercommunication Is the Villain

Research shows that the more employees know about the reasons for management's actions, the more favorably they view them as compared with employees who feel uninformed. In an *Industry Week* article discussing the communication problems involved in company mergers, consultant John R. Purser laid out useful guidelines that can apply just as well to any restructuring situation:

1. Develop a detailed communication plan after analyzing needs.
2. Communicate to all audiences and constituencies that have an interest in the restructuring, such as customers, the financial community, news media, and, of course, employees.
3. Coordinate all communications to these audiences to ensure that employees don't learn news from some outside source.
4. Establish a schedule of communications and stick to it.
5. Be candid, even if it hurts.
6. Be as completely accurate as you can—backtracking with "clarification" is no way to build confidence.
7. Take the time to be visible. Visit plants and offices, and hold department or shift meetings.
8. Consider conducting a confidential employee opinion survey shortly after the restructuring has taken place. It can reveal vital concerns that management might otherwise overlook.

This last recommendation is vitally important. A major problem, maintains Hay Group's Peter Gelfond, is that most company managements think that immediately after a restructuring is a bad time to survey their employees. Wrong, says Gelfond:

> When times are bad, when there's been a lot of chaos, that's the time to survey. That's when you get the red flags that tell you what's gone wrong with the restructuring. What are the things that are making quality worse now? Why is the productivity dropping? Is there too much duplication of effort? Has the work flow been disrupted? And when we find out, how do we resolve it?

Communicating—Navy Style

Robert J. Fierle, president and chairman of American Precision Industries, Inc., believes a company must keep its employees realistically informed during a downsizing to prevent wild speculation. He illustrates his point vividly with a wartime analogy: how navy commanders kept sailors informed during World War II.

> When you got aboard ship, a day or so out at sea the captain would open the orders and then tell you up front the probability of your coming back alive. "If you've got any unfinished business, send your letters home, make out your will, get it done now." The sailors could handle this better than rumors, which were always worse than the reality anyway. At least they were prepared emotionally. So why not level with your employees and say, "Here are your odds," rather than keep them totally in the dark?

TEMPER THE TRAUMA

Let's face it—terminating employees is a dirty job. There's no way to make it pleasant. But if it has to be done, there are ways to minimize the pain and suffering. Beyond humane considerations, there are very practical reasons:

- The organization will have a better climate for getting on with the job of revitalizing itself.
- Its reputation as a company that shows respect and concern for its employees will be enhanced—an important factor when there comes a time to hire new talent. It pays to be admired rather than despised. Merck & Company, which in 1990 was named the most admired U.S. company by *Fortune* magazine and one of the 10 best companies for working mothers by *Working Mother* magazine, says such accolades have helped to bring in over 100,000 applications for jobs in New Jersey alone.

- The key performers you wish to retain will be less prone to start circulating their résumés if the downsizing process is handled humanely.

Parting: Sweet Sorrow or Sour Grapes?

Here are some guidelines that companies can follow to alleviate the bitter impact on displaced managers—and just as important, positively influence the attitudes, motivation, and commitment of those who remain.

• *Early-retirement windows.* Such packages are the most common form of voluntary work force reduction. They are usually offered with various sweeteners: full benefits even when the employee has not reached regular retirement age, adding five years to the employee's age and job tenure, a substantial bonus cash settlement, social security supplement, extension of health and life benefits, or outplacement assistance for those who want to continue working.

Although the early-retirement option is probably the most humane approach to downsizing—aside from relying on normal attrition, which is too slow for most organizations—we've already pointed out that it can have serious disadvantages as well, one of them being that an organization can lose some of its best people if they take advantage of the offer. There are also serious cost implications: the medical insurance premiums for retirees younger than 65, who are not yet qualified for Medicare, can be burdensome and sometimes crippling to a company. And in this era of wildly escalating medical-care costs, these premiums sharply increase every year.

To avoid losing people they want to keep, some companies are focusing their early-retirement offers more narrowly than they did in the past. IBM is one of them. Under its voluntary retirement program offered in late 1989, each IBM facility was to tailor the program to its own specific strategic needs. Employees with critical skills—such as programmers—may not be able to take advantage of the offer.

To be successful, early-retirement packages should meet several requirements:

1. There should be no coercion involved. For example, the window for employees to decide on whether to accept the offer should be long enough to avoid the appearance of rushing a crucial, complex life decision.
2. Any pattern of discrimination should be avoided. If the package offered happens to cover a predominance of minorities or women, the employer can look forward to costly lawsuits.
3. The early-retirement program must be communicated thoroughly. Individual retirement counseling, financial planning assistance, and telephone hot lines will help employees make an informed decision.

• *Generous severance packages.* Downsizing companies often offer richer severance payments than they would in ordinary circumstances. For example, an employee who would normally receive one month's severance pay might receive three months' pay during a substantial downsizing. Perhaps the most generous package was offered by Polaroid when it downsized: Managers over 50 years of age received one month's pay for each year of service.

More typical is the severance allowance formula developed by New Jersey Bell for its management employees. Based on a sliding scale tied to length of service, the program provides 1 week of severance pay per year of service up to 4 years, then 5 weeks of pay for 4 years, 7 weeks pay for 5 years, and so on, with a ceiling of 17 weeks of salary.

But some companies are going well beyond such conventional approaches to severance pay. An example is the program of Armstrong World Industries, Inc., maker of flooring and home furnishings. Called the "Employee Protection Plan for Salaried Employees," the program was described by *CFO* magazine:

> Dubbed a "tin parachute" by those in the compensation business, Armstrong's plan protects all salaried employees at the

parent company in case of a change in control in much the same way golden parachutes have traditionally protected top management. If Armstrong employees lose their jobs within two years of a change in control for reasons other than cause, or if they voluntarily quit for good reason (such as a lowered salary or a dramatically changed job description), they're covered by the tin parachute. The plan entitles an employee to a severance package that becomes increasingly generous based on his or her years of service. For instance, employees who had worked at Armstrong for five years would receive five weeks' salary if they lost their jobs because of a change in control; but those who had worked for 25 years would get 75 weeks of salary. Employees are also entitled to continued health and life insurance benefits, again based on length of service, up to a maximum of one year.

"Our philosophy in setting up this plan was to protect our employees from what's happening out there in the business world," says Thomas Roy, director of compensation for Armstrong.

Eastman Kodak announced a similar program early in 1990, designed not only to ease employee concerns about the company's restructuring but also to discourage takeover attempts. The plan includes a lump-sum termination allowance ranging from six weeks' to two years' pay, continuation of health and life insurance for four months to a year, a full share of any wage dividend declared in the year in which employment ends, and outplacement assistance and a retraining allowance of as much as $5,000.

Résumé workshops, personal counseling, and skills enhancement training are some other possibilities that downsizing employers should consider.

• *Free outplacement services.* As U.S. businesses have sharply downsized, the outplacement industry has correspondingly *upsized,* growing about 30 percent a year. In the American Management Association's 1989 survey of downsizing activity, 67.9 percent of companies planning to downsize within a year said they would provide outplacement services for some or all departing employees. Good outplacement services can go a long way toward easing the transition from unemployment to another job or career. But although the concept of outplacement services is highly recommendable, it is not always beneficial in actual practice. Many companies appear to retain outplacement firms more as a sop to their consciences than as a genuine effort to help their ex-employees find good new jobs—and the outplacement services vary widely in quality.

The competence of an outplacement agency depends, of course, on the quality and experience level of its staff. Since a firm may be retained at times to handle very large numbers of departing employees (as was the case when IBM retained Drake Beam Morin in the late 1980s), it may be hard pressed to supply an adequate level of service.

That is one reason that a company should not simply turn its displaced managers over to an outplacement firm and then forget about them. To actually help former employees, a company must first select a top-quality outplacement firm and then closely monitor the firm's efforts until its former employees find jobs elsewhere or make other plans. A good example is Mobil's downsizing in the middle 1980s. Mobil's Elizabeth Julia Cole recalls that she spent many weeks evaluating outplacement firms before several were selected, then worked closely with them for eight months while they provided services for departing managers.

A full-service outplacement firm should be able to:

- Provide immediate on-site support at the time of separation.
- Tailor its services to the individual manager's needs rather than using a cookie-cutter approach.
- Provide the displaced employee with a career reemployment action plan based on an assessment of the individual's goals, objectives, interests, skills, abilities, and income requirements.
- When needed, teach job-search skills, such as résumé writing, interviewing techniques, job-offer evaluation, and employment negotiations.

• Provide office support services: desk space, personal stationery, use of a telephone and message center, access to typing and mailing services, résumé printing, and research facilities.

• *Redeploy employees whose jobs have been eliminated.* Looking for redeployment opportunities should be a top priority for management when it downsizes. Unfortunately, too many companies overlook this approach to minimizing the number of people who must be laid off. Some firms, however, have found that redeployment is a practical way not only to make downsizing more humane, but also to meet specific staffing needs.

Texas Instruments, Inc.'s operation in Johnson City, Tennessee, is an outstanding example. In 1989 Kenneth V. Spenser, vice president of the information technology group, recognized that the division's eight layers of management were hampering its ability to respond quickly enough to the competition. In some cases, managers had only two people reporting to them.

Spenser moved fast, and by late 1989 the management/supervisor team had been cut down from 240 to 103. But, remarkably, he did it without unleashing a torrent of pink slips. Most of the displaced managers were redeployed to the technical and engineering jobs from which they had come. They did not sacrifice their chances for career advancement because the division also made changes in its "technical ladder." With more rungs on the ladder—ranging from associate engineer to senior fellow—there were far more advancement opportunities. And, observes Spenser, "At the top of the technical ladder you can make as much money as any vice president in the corporation."

• *Sensitivity to departing employees.* Nothing can be more important than to treat terminated employees as individuals with worth, rather than as surplus scrap. This means allowing them to leave with dignity, giving them a chance to say farewells to their colleagues, listening to the feelings they want to express. Management often seems to forget that humiliating termination methods not only exacerbate the bitterness of job loss, but tell *surviving* employees something about how much the company values them as human beings. The impact on morale can be devastating.

It is especially critical to give terminated employees individual attention. Grow Group, Inc., was very aware of this when it downsized in 1988. Teresa E. McCaslin, now vice president of human resources for Avery, was then Grow Group's vice president of human resources and administration. She describes how her department dealt with terminated employees:

> When we had to cut 30 percent of our corporate staff, we developed written, individual packages for every terminated employee describing the severance arrangements. We gave them each their written package to look over, and set up an appointment for the next day. A human resources staffer talked to each person individually for anywhere from thirty minutes to an hour, to explain what the package meant and how it would affect the employee personally. Though disappointed that things had worked out this way, they understood because they knew exactly what was going on. They could leave with their heads high, because they knew that they were not being dismissed because of poor performance; it was strictly related to the financial condition of the company and the restructuring that we were forced into. Although they did feel betrayed in a sense, they didn't feel that the company betrayed them, but that *business* had betrayed them. One employee said to me, "Personally I don't feel now like you're just slamming the door in my face and putting me out on the street without doing the best you can for me."

WORK WITH SURVIVORS

Even when the hard decisions have been made and the affected employees have left, downsizing is not complete. Now it's necessary to regroup—and to redeploy the people who remain so that they can most effectively enable the organization to attain its goals. Long-term success comes not from off-loading human resources but from enabling them to realize their potential. As Robert Tomasko notes in *Downsizing,* it is critically important in downsized companies that managers create a new culture to help fill the vacuum created by departed employees.

Time and time again in our research we ran into cases where the problems of remaining employees were ignored— even when *displaced* employees were treated fairly well. Many companies don't realize that downsizing can be traumatic for survivors as well as for job losers. The impact is different but is often just as severe.

Companies can take several steps to reduce this impact and help survivors adjust to a new world. Here are some recommendations:

• *Acknowledge the mourning stage.* There's an understandable temptation for the president to get up right after the downsizing and lead the cheers: "Okay, folks, now away we go." But that's often done too soon, and it fails to acknowledge that people are deeply upset over the fact that colleagues who have been sitting next to them for years are now gone (and that maybe in the next wave they'll be gone too). Top management must be willing to say, "We know it doesn't feel good now. We understand the sense of loss and that's okay. We accept that."

• *Give people a chance to articulate their feelings.* After the frightening San Francisco earthquake in October 1989, scores of teachers, mental health workers, and other professionals helped Bay Area residents get hold of themselves. Those seeking help were all told: Talk about it. That's a good prescription for downsizing survivors, too. Management should give them a chance to articulate their feelings of insecurity and stress, rather than pretend they don't exist. This allows employees to work out their emotional reactions to the changes in the workplace and get on with the business of running the company.

• *Hold more informational meetings.* The more news—even if some of it is bad news—that management shares with survivors the better. Frequent meetings also give management an opportunity to focus on the future of the organization (while not ignoring or denying what has happened in the recent past). Above all, management must never try to give reassurances about the future that are unrealistic. This is a period during which employee trust in management is fragile at best—and credibility lost at this point may take years to regain. Hence it is important to go beyond simply disseminating or sharing information; it is also essential to understand how that information is being heard, interpreted, and internalized.

Right Associates' Richard Chagnon refers to working with survivors as "revitalization" or "building new commitments." Although primarily an outplacement firm that helps laid-off employees to find other jobs or careers, Right Associates is also developing "performance management or enhancement" programs that focus on helping surviving managers become more productive and gain more satisfaction from their jobs. This involves a number of actions:

> First, the company must revisit its mission and strategic directions. When a company restructures, something serious has happened to it. Business cannot go on exactly as before. Strategic direction has changed in fact, if not on paper. Unless you determine how you are going to manage the new situation, and then convey the new direction to all of your employees, you will fall victim to recreating by instinct the very same conditions that created the original crisis.
> You must let them know the banner under which you're now flying. You must define the specific areas on which the company's energies are now to be focused. This could be a change in product strategy, a different marketing approach, a program to raise quality standards.
> The main point is that the survivors need a new focus in order to understand what the new company is now about, and where they can make their best contribution.

Hay Group's Peter Gelfond finds that many companies leave their middle managers in a state of limbo after a restructuring—and he recommends that top management pay far more attention to its better performers unless it wants to lose them.

During restructurings such as mergers, individual managers must be treated with respect or their morale will drop to zero. Let's say I'm a middle manager and I have a boss I've worked with for five years. I've aligned myself to this boss and I trust him (or her). All of a sudden there's a merger and they switch bosses on me. Now that's OK, as long as the new senior manager really spends time with me and explains to me what's going to happen to my career. But often that doesn't happen. The senior managers themselves may not feel good about what's happened, because they had people they related to and now they've been dealt a whole new cast of characters. In this situation, the middle managers may be left out to dry. They're just sitting there; nobody's communicating with them. They don't know if they have a career any more and they start thinking about looking somewhere else. To deal with this, the organization must first identify its top performers and potential superstars among middle managers. Get to them first and let them know it's okay. You've initially got to get to your better performers because they're the ones who can pick up the phone and call a headhunter. Over time, get to the other managers. It's not easy for senior managers to do this, because they're in chaos, too. But they've got to make the effort, or key people will turn sour.

THERE IS A CHOICE

Every restructuring situation is different. But in almost all cases, management has a choice:

- It can restructure in such a way that morale plummets, commitment evaporates, mistrust of management escalates, and organizational performance takes a nosedive.
- Or it can plan and implement its restructuring so as to minimize the pain and suffering, maintain morale and credibility, leave the organization leaner but not

weaker, and stimulate the energy needed to achieve long-term goals.

Whichever alternative an organization chooses, it is inevitable that the role of managers after the restructuring will undergo profound changes. We'll consider those changes in the next chapter.

CHAPTER 7

REMAKING THE MANAGER: NEW ROLES TO MEET NEW CHALLENGES

The only real replacement for today's manager is tomorrow's more competent manager with broader, deeper capabilities. The future manager won't look or be the same. He'll change in response to persistent pressures from the management environment and from inside the management process. Once the iron hand of structural tradition is relaxed, a whole host of new channels for communication, evaluation, supervision, and negotiation comes into view. Perhaps the most startling effect will be an increase in organizational flexibility and the pace of organizational change. Effective managers will become "change engineers," especially competent in planning and arranging organizational invention, innovation, and modification.

—Sound like the latest thoughts of a hot management guru? Wrong. It's from an article written back in 1966 by management professor Dale Yoder.

So what's the point? Simply that none of the many "revolutionary" ideas about the manager of the future are really that new. They've been around for years, but they've been honored mostly in the breach. Long ago, when the United States dominated world markets, there was little pressure to change the ways that managers managed. But now there's an almost desperate urgency about putting these concepts into practice. One reason is the onset of brutal global competition. Today, managerial change is mandatory for survival.

Other factors also make it imperative for U.S. managers to function differently:

- Technological advances—particularly in information and communication technology—are making many traditional managerial roles obsolete.
- Persistent organizational downsizing has permanently altered the jobs of the managers who survive.
- The need for faster decisions, faster product development, faster production, and faster marketing requires radical new approaches to managing.
- The rapidly increasing diversity of the U.S. work force requires new people skills from managers.
- The trend toward the autonomous workplace means managers can no longer rely on the "command-and-control" techniques of the past.

But when it comes to doing something about the urgent need for transforming managerial functions, we've got a big problem—literally. Huge, complex organizations don't remake themselves quickly. Even smaller organizations find it difficult to help their managers develop new skills and new approaches. But just try it in General Motors, which one GM manager described as "a big blob that has a mind of its own and just kind of moves" (Or, perhaps, doesn't move.) Leaders may *talk* about driving decisions downward, but talk doesn't produce meaningful change. Indeed, talk without action causes voluntary deafness.

Yet so far there has been more talk than action—by both top management and middle managers. It is top management's responsibility to instigate the needed changes, get solidly behind them, and provide the means for implementing them. Middle managers bear the responsibility of accepting the need for change and being willing to relearn ways of doing things even if it means stress, discomfort, and reorientation—because that's what the change process is all about. At the same time, change presents golden opportunities for creating more job satisfaction and more job challenge.

This is a most critical aspect of the new partnership between middle managers and their companies. The very word *partnership* represents a radical shift from the old paternalistic relationship that prevailed for so many years. Traditionally, helping managers develop the skills they needed to perform effectively was a one-way process controlled by the company. Managers were the passive recipients of whatever development programs the company decided to provide. The result of this unilateral development approach was often no development. Managers recognized that they had to go through the motions of participating in the programs that were offered. But because the relationship of the manager to the company was more child-parent than partner-partner, many managers simply did not buy into the development programs. Real change was not achieved for two major reasons:

- Managers had very little input into identifying their own development needs and planning how to deal with them.
- What managers learned in development programs often did not jibe with the actual culture of their organization, making it impossible for them to implement suggested approaches to managing.

Can managers learn new skills and new behaviors? Yes, but their companies must first make a genuine commitment to the partnership concept. This means giving managers more of a share in the planning and implementation of their own development. Doing so can significantly help managers to buy into the need for radical changes in the way they manage.

THAWING THE FROZEN ORGANIZATION

As with any change process, accepting and learning new managerial roles can be hampered by resistance from managers. In fact, some senior executives believe that the major stumbling block to actualizing the "new manager" is the "old manager." But although managers have often been blamed for failing to change their ways, much of the responsibility for the problem lies elsewhere: with top management's failure to create—or even *permit*—an organizational environment in which the "new manager" can thrive and flourish. Managers who are asked to change their style when the organizational system is frozen into the status quo will find themselves frustrated and blocked even if they are *willing* to change.

Training and development are indispensable in fostering the desired changes, but by themselves they cannot do the job. Other major conditions must be present:

• As with any other organizational programs, solutions imposed from the top are often resisted. For managers to buy into the change program, they must be given some input into its design and planning.

• Management's credibility is based not on what it *says* are the behaviors it wants from its managers, but on whether or not it *rewards* those behaviors. That means management must develop a system by which these behaviors are rated and used as criteria for both rewards and sanctions.

• Although managers may make changes in their style, they will soon slip back into their old ways of doing things *unless they find that their new behaviors are effective.* If managers are stifled and frustrated by a rigid, go-by-the-book organizational environment, they will soon conclude that it just doesn't pay to change. For example, top management may typically say: "We want managers who set their own personal standards of performance at the highest level, understand that change is needed, can adapt and be flexible to that need, will take initiative, will take reasonable risks, will take responsibility for their own decisions." But when managers try to live up to these requirements, they find that they are squelched at every turn. They may understandably become bitter about what they see as top-management incompetence compounded by hypocrisy. The upshot: Managers go back to the old behaviors—going by the book and doing the safe thing. For example, a manager quoted by Leonard W. Johnson and Alan L. Frohman said:

> Management tells us they want to move decisions down to our level. It's just lip service. The first time we determined which outside supplier to use, our bosses reversed our decision, saying we were not aware of a critical factor—there were provisions in the labor agreement with the unions which restricted our ability to outsource those parts. Why didn't they give us the full picture in the first place?

Training managers in new patterns of behavior without creating the organizational systems needed to make this behavior effective is a waste of time and money—and, worse, severely demotivating. For example, if managers are asked to make decisions that were formerly made further up the line, they must be able to obtain the information necessary for making those decisions. If there are no mechanisms in place for getting this information, they'll lose interest and long for the good old days when these decisions were made by somebody else.

A BOTTOM-LINE APPROACH TO TRAINING AND DEVELOPMENT

In a 1989 survey of 101 human resources executives done by ODI, an international management consulting and training firm, 76 percent of the respondents said they would devote more time to "preparing managers and employees to cope with rapid change" during the 1990s. At the same time, 83 percent said that "making the human resource function more accountable for impacting the bottom line" will become more important in their company.

These answers pinpoint a major obstacle to achieving managerial change. True, we now have "human resources" departments when we used to have "personnel" departments. But has anything really changed besides the name? Aren't these departments perceived by top management as providing administrative services that may contribute to overhead but certainly not to profits? That's one reason downsizing often hits the human resources department harder than others—it is considered a cost rather than a contributor. And yet, unless companies invest the money and effort required to develop the kinds of managers needed during the 1990s, they'll find themselves slipping still further behind in the competitive race.

Consultant Franck de Chambeau points out that many companies establish their business strategy first and *then* belatedly bring human resources into the picture. As a result, the strategy often doesn't work. The human resources department must be a *partner* in strategic thinking, not an afterthought. Companies need a new mind-set to integrate the management of all their assets: financial, informational, technological, and *human*.

Both top management and human resources professionals can take the initiative in implementing this crucial shift in emphasis from "administrative" services to "strategic" services. Human resources people can influence their own image in a number of ways. One is by emphasizing their planning, problem-solving, and advising functions and reducing emphasis on their administrative functions. Another is to clearly relate their activities to the bottom line.

James Ryan, director of Welch's human resources, believes it is up to HR people to persuade top management that there are long-term bottom-line benefits from spending money on training and developing middle managers to assume new roles. When he joined his company, the human resources department limited its activities to keeping records, negotiating labor agreements, and keeping the company out of legal trouble. The budget for management development was $20,000.

Now, five years later, the budget approaches $200,000 and is expected to increase over the next several years. Ryan describes the approach he used to convince top management that the investment would be worthwhile:

> The first step is to identify deficiencies that exist now. Go out in the organization. Talk with people in all functions: administrative, support, operating. Ask them what they'd like to see improved—how human resources can help their part of the organization be more responsive to the marketplace and to the needs of the operation.
>
> With that as a basis, conduct a formal needs analysis. Take the results to the CEO and say, "These are the things we can address by training and development, and the return on this investment will be reduced turnover, increased efficiency, improved productivity." Point out what it costs to replace a middle manager. Put it on a bottom-line basis: Not because it's "nice" to do but because it will benefit the organization in tangible ways.

For their own contribution, top managements can help human resources professionals develop the skills and acquire the stature to take a more aggressive strategic role. Among the steps recommended by behavioral scientist Celeste Coruzzi of W. Warner Burke Associates, are:

- Increasing the pool of HR generalists.
- Integrating HR strategic planning into the business planning cycle.
- Creating management development programs for HR professionals, including feedback on their performance from line managers.
- Training HR professionals to perform the role of consultant—for example, training in the use of diagnostic models to guide their investigations and methods for creating large-scale change.

CHOOSING NEW MANAGERS: SELECT, DON'T SETTLE

A major challenge facing employers today is to help their *current* managers redefine their jobs and learn new approaches to managing. But equally important is selecting *new* managers, with a different set of criteria than companies have used in the past.

Traditionally, management people rose through the ranks because they were technically proficient. Managerial ability was extrapolated from superiority in skills that actually had nothing to do with managing. As a result, many employees were promoted to be managers who were wrong for the role. They ended up being either ineffectual or downright destructive.

This approach to choosing managers was damaging enough when organizations functioned in a relatively stable environment. In today's pressure-cooker environment, which requires highly developed managerial skills, choosing managers for their technical skills alone can be suicidal.

Some companies are beginning to realize this. Teresa E. McCaslin, former vice president of human resources and administration for Grow Group, Inc., describes the approach that the company takes to ensure a sound selection of managers:

> We recognized that some people have management potential and others don't, regardless of their technical talent. Often, good managers today don't even have the technical skills of the people reporting to them, but they are leaders.
>
> We are segmenting employees who will always be A-one technically but will never be managers no matter what kind of training they receive. We measure that through a performance review system, talking to supervisors, subordinates, peers, and just watching people and asking: "How do they manage—are they developing people, are they looked up to by others in the organization? Are they better just working

by themselves, because they like to go off by themselves and not be part of teams?"

Then you have a second category of those who will probably make it as managers, but they will need extensive management awareness training.

Finally, you have your born leaders. They just get in there and know how to set priorities, what to do, and how to bring the best out in their people.

What qualities should a company look for in its managers today? When you consider the roles that managers today must play, the following qualities seem to be critical. The manager must be able—and *willing*—to:

- Focus outward and "read" the environment.
- Think strategically.
- Be flexible.
- Take risks.
- Be innovative.
- Make decisions quickly without "paralysis by analysis."
- Approach new ideas positively.
- Communicate effectively—both sending and receiving.
- Conduct win-win negotiations skillfully.
- Manage—and *create*—change.
- Delegate effectively.
- Cross organizational lines (and walls) with ease.
- Turn data into useful information.
- Assess information quickly.
- Share information rather than hoard it.

FOCUSING ON THE KEY PROBLEM AREAS

Global competition, the flatter organization, demographic work force trends, and fast-moving technology all require fresh responses from today's managers. Companies that have tried to help their managers learn new roles have pinpointed key areas where intense development and training are needed.

Developing a Global Perspective

Right Associates' Richard Chagnon put it this way:

> Managers need to be more global, because our economy is integrally connected to the different economies around the world. The 1987 stock market "swoon," as one newscaster put it, made us realize how closely everything is tied together around the world. This means that every manager must be working with a realization of that global impact. For example, the manager of purchasing will be buying from the global market, and must know what is happening around the globe.

Persuading managers to adopt a global perspective is far from easy—particularly in companies where the perspective has been traditionally parochial. One such company is Welch's, the Massachusetts-based fruit juice company that also makes jams and jellies. Welch's was once a low-pressure company that faced relatively little competition in its field. All that has changed. As consumer tastes have shifted from soft drinks to more natural drinks, the juice business has skyrocketed, bringing some major players into the market, such as Coke Foods, Seneca, and Treetop. To become more competitive in this combative environment, Welch's consolidated and closed some operations. In addition, it entered the global arena by expanding its market into Japan.

Senior management at Welch's recognized that the new pressures on the organization meant that its managers would have to develop a far broader perspective than they had previously. Most of the managers were local people who had never been expected to know much beyond their specific jobs. Jim Ryan, Welch's director of human resources, says:

> Our middle managers are very competent functionally—but they have lacked the broad perspective that is necessary for them to be total business contributors. Now we are training them intensively to broaden their horizons. Here's what we're telling them: We want you to have a broad perspective, not only of our business, but of business in general. We want you

to understand the dynamics of the domestic market, to understand what the global economy is going to mean to our business, to recognize Europe 1992 and the opportunities it presents, and to see how important the Pacific Rim will be to the future global economic climate.

We tie our educational programs into our corporate vision, and then we discuss how managers can translate their activities into a pattern and a strategy consistent with that vision.

A critically important aspect of broadening the perspective of today's managers is to educate them to include the customer in their thinking. Managers must learn to design their operations to focus on fulfilling customer needs—not just the company's priorities or the priorities of their department.

Letting Go: It's Not Easy to Stop Being the "Boss"

In today's flatter organization, authority is drawn down the line toward the point of production and the delivery of service. Managers must learn to relinquish authority to more autonomous employees who now make decisions they previously bucked upstairs. General Electric chairman Jack Welch says, "Managers have to see their roles as a combination of teacher, cheerleader, and liberator, not controller."

That isn't easy for many managers to accept. They have problems with their new roles of empowering employees. They resent losing control over information and resources and being bypassed, as some of them see it, in the process of increasing employee involvement. And they have trouble accepting the increasing ambiguity of hierarchical roles and authority/responsibility relationships. Nor is a manager who is already overloaded with work necessarily happy about the added responsibility of negotiating decision-making boundaries with "subordinates."

Many managers believe that there is a finite amount of power in an organization. Therefore, if somebody else gets more power, that means they lose some. They don't buy the concept that they really acquire more power—and influence—by empowering others.

Management professor and author Rosabeth Moss Kanter says that managers can feel loss of power in their new roles because they don't always know what their people are doing. Often subordinates may bypass them and interact directly with other decision makers inside and outside the company. Some employees may sit in on high-level strategy meetings to which their managers were not invited. This can have a devastating effect on managers with insecure egos.

Today's widespread use of computers also acts to weaken managerial authority. In 1985 there was one computer terminal for every five white-collar employees—by 1990, there was one for every three. And by 2000, predicts The Gartner Group, a Connecticut-based market-research firm, the number of personal computers in offices is expected to quadruple to 46 million.

This trend will have a profound impact on traditional forms of authority. According to Shoshana Zuboff, author and associate professor at the Harvard Business School: "Since managers are no longer the guardians of the knowledge base, we do not need the command-control type of executive."

Yet many managers firmly believe that unless they exert strict controls over their subordinates, the work won't get done. They feel that the way to motivate and direct behavior is to exercise control through authority. These managers seek compliance through hierarchical and economic pressures, including fear.

Interestingly enough, a study of productivity and managerial style made back in the early 1960s by the University of Michigan showed that such managers usually had low-producing departments. Management author and motivation expert Saul W. Gellerman summarized the results of the study this way:

Low-Producing Managers:

- Rigidly imposed production goals on their subordinates.
- Directed employee behavior by minutely organizing each job, exactly prescribing methods, and setting rigid standards.
- Often tried to cajole employees into working harder with artificial "human relations" techniques, tried to turn work into a game with contests and other manipulative devices, or used the threat of dismissal or demotion as their main motivating device.
- Placed more importance on controlling the *conduct* of their subordinates than on controlling the *results* achieved.

High-Producing Managers:

- Supported the "psychological advantage" of their subordinates by letting them do their work in their own way.
- Set general goals and standards.
- Expected their subordinates to do their work effectively and used measurements largely to find out where there were problems they could help resolve.
- Were more interested in controlling the *results* achieved by their subordinates than in controlling their *conduct*.

Companies must face the fact that some managers will *never* make the adjustment from one managerial style to the other. As Robert J. Fierle, president and chairman of American Precision Industries, puts it:

Many managers will find it difficult to sit down and have dialogue with the people on the floor and be receptive to their suggestions. The mind-set of most managers is, "I know more than anyone who works for me." So managers may look at this as a threat. But it's absolutely vital for them to change. They have to make the transition from straw boss to communicator, listener, and leader.

It takes a long time to change such ingrained culture, and in some cases it won't happen. In our own company, we may have to shift some middle managers to spots where they can use their technical expertise but don't have to exert listening and leadership skills. Younger managers are embracing new concepts better than older ones. They seem to understand that if an employee comes to them with a good idea that makes the job cost less or makes it go faster or improves quality, it will reflect positively on them. One young manager said to me, "I figure I'm not losing a flag from my lapel, I'm actually getting another one."

What can management do to facilitate this kind of change? The most important action is to sit down and openly discuss the problem with those who are having difficulty adjusting to a new relationship with their subordinates. Welch's human resources manager, Jim Ryan, says this has been effective in his company:

> Some of our managers felt very insecure with the idea of relinquishing some of their power. They felt that it would diminish their responsibilities in the eyes of their boss. Our response has been to spend some time coaching and counseling them. We talk about their concerns and problems and encourage the participants to help one another resolve them.
>
> We try to convince them that by releasing some of their authority they will be even more important to the organization. They won't be directing their people as much—instead, they will be establishing broad parameters within which their people will work to make sure we've got the right quality specs, we're achieving efficiency and productivity targets. The managers will be available to help with problems as they arise, but they won't be out there looking over their subordinates' shoulders, pointing out mistakes, and telling them how to improve the operation.
>
> We believe our approach has been generally effective, although not every manager has accepted the change process.

But most are less concerned now about "not being as important as I was before." They're beginning to recognize the difference between traditional management and leadership. Managers tell, leaders suggest and solicit ideas and comments—they encourage questions. When mistakes and uncertainties develop, leaders are there not with a whip but with a concern for using mistakes to create better people.

As Jim Ryan found out, these are not easy concepts for managers to accept. At the heart of the matter is what kind of authority makes a job important. In one sense, maintains management writer Arthur H. Kuriloff, managers are not giving up authority at all—they are simply replacing one kind of authority with another. One is based on hierarchical control, while the other is based on group-centered leadership that encourages exchange of ideas between leader and group, with the leader acting as mentor and coach. Together, leader and group adopt work procedures, establish goals, and assess achievement.

In practicing group-centered leadership, managers are not giving up their authority but are shifting emphasis to a different *source* for their authority. That source is now their ability to command the acceptance and cooperation of their group. While their bureaucratic power may be slipping away, they can increase their leadership power. This is a tougher challenge, of course, because they can no longer use their vested authority as a substitute for real leadership. They must create their own authority.

Helping managers make this difficult transition is an imperative for any organization that wants to push decision making downward. One mistake that many companies make is to assume that only nonmanagerial employees need to learn new skills and behaviors in a changing organizational environment. These companies believe that managers will successfully adapt to change without additional training and support.

The result: Managers become obstacles to change rather than change facilitators. One example of this is provided by the Harley-Davidson Motorcycle Company. Almost run off the road by Japanese competition in the early 1980s, the only surviving U.S. motorcycle company decided to fight back by adopting some of the very methods with which the Japanese produced high-quality machines at lower prices. These methods included employee involvement—giving plant workers more control over their own jobs. One of the techniques Harley introduced was statistical operator control (SOC), which permitted each employee to monitor the quality of his or her work with statistical charts.

Harley's middle managers felt threatened by this radical change. They "owned" quality—that was their domain. Now they saw ownership of quality shifting away from them to the employees who worked directly on the product. The whole idea that *everyone* should continuously improve the process and that plant operators could use statistics shook up and scared quite a few middle managers.

The SOC program ran into trouble because Harley-Davidson neglected to prepare its middle managers for changes that threatened their authority. Once it recognized the problem it acted to reduce middle management resistance. Middle managers were trained in the continuous improvement philosophy and SOC methodology. This helped to gain acceptance for the program, but there was still resistance by some managers. That resistance was addressed through coaching and having middle managers participate in team problem-solving activities so that they would feel like part of the process. Harley-Davidson is now a highly successful company that has recaptured most of its lost market share.

Telling Off the Boss

One interesting approach to changing managerial styles is gaining favor in some progressive companies: evaluation of managers by their peers or subordinates. Mass Mutual Insurance has embarked on such a program under the leadership of CEO Tom Wheeler. To be successful, he says, the process must begin at the top: The CEO must be willing to be evaluated by the officers who report to him or her. Wheeler says:

> This is a program we are driving down to all our managers. Based on the evaluation results, we are devising remedial programs to help us work on the areas that need strengthening. But it won't work unless the chief executive is willing to go through it, too. Our managers aren't going to do it willingly if they ask my reporting managers, "Well, did you evaluate Wheeler?" and the answer is no. If I don't do it, I can't ask the rest of the company to do it. And that wasn't easy for me, because like many CEOs I've spent a career trying to please my boss and saying I really don't care what the people below think of me.

Xerox is another company that utilizes assessments of managers' behavior by their people as part of a program to improve their managerial styles. Xerox's Reprographic Business Group—which is responsible for the research design, production, and delivery of copiers and duplicators—embarked on its Management Style Change Strategy program in an effort to encourage more work force participation in an environment of openness and trust. To accomplish more participation, management realized, would require some dramatic changes in the behavior of managers who had grown up under the "command and control" system.

The program had five basic elements:

1. Identifying specific behaviors characteristic of an effective management style for the Reprographic Business Group (*see box*).
2. Giving managers feedback on how they performed against these specific behaviors.
3. Supporting managers in change planning and implementation of their plans.

4. Providing periodic feedback to managers on their performance against the desired behaviors.
5. Encouraging managers to share the results of their performance with their workers and supervisors to help improve their management practices.

Xerox management was encouraged by the results of the program after three years. Employees' ratings of their managers improved significantly on a scale of one to five. The improvements were not spectacular, but as Xerox executives point out, changing the management style of nearly 1,000 managers is a slow task requiring commitment and patience on the part of the top management team. The executives believe, however, that the change process is being facilitated by their formal program allowing workers to appraise their managers about how they manage.

Working with People: What Xerox Wants from Its Managers

When it began its Management Style Strategy Program, Xerox's human resources staff sought input on desirable management behaviors from a variety of sources: top management, nonmanagerial employees, management training participants, and consultants. The staff ended up with a list of 44 specific behaviors in five broad categories. These behaviors are observable, measurable, and specific enough to allow employees to assess their managers' strengths and weaknesses—yet they are not so specific that they unduly constrain managers' natural individualism. A good manager, according to the program,

Employee Involvement

1. Involves employees in discussions about work-related issues.
2. Utilizes employees' skills and individual strengths.
3. Solicits ideas from employees.
4. Guides team decisions to match overall organizational objectives.
5. Helps teams develop a common understanding of the problems and objectives they face.
6. Involves employees in decision making.

Working with People (continued)

7. Encourages employees toward cooperation rather than competition.
8. Establishes a climate of openness and trust.

Task Management

9. Discusses with employees the objectives of and problems with their assignments.
10. Seeks employees' input on how resource limitations will affect the accomplishment of their tasks.
11. Reviews employees' goals, timetables, and accomplishments as needed.
12. Clarifies with employees the results expected from their assignments.
13. Indicates the highest priority assignments.
14. Seeks employees' input on their current workload and competing priorities before giving them additional assignments.
15. Provides feedback about the aspects of employees' assignments that they handled well.
16. Provides feedback to employees upon completion of their assignments about how they could have improved their performance.

Communication

17. Listens to employees' ideas and concerns without interrupting.
18. Encourages employees to speak.
19. Asks employees to clarify areas about which they are unsure or concerned.
20. Summarizes what employees have said to verify their understanding.
21. Seeks input from employees about decisions that affect them.
22. Provides information to employees which affects their ability to perform assignments.
23. Shares general business information with employees.
24. Initiates two-way communication with employees.
25. Gets to know employees as individuals.
26. Maintains personal contact with employees.

Working with People (continued)

People Development

27. Discusses with employees their strengths and weaknesses.
28. Works with employees to improve their performance.
29. Provides opportunities for employees to develop beyond their present capabilities.
30. Helps employees understand how their work activities and responsibilities contribute to their organization.

Leadership

31. Adjusts his or her management approach to meet individual employees' needs.
32. Manages employees differently from task to task based on their experience, job knowledge, and ability.
33. Involves employees in planning and implementing changes that affect them.
34. Seeks employees' commitment and support for such changes.
35. Implements changes with a minimum of confusion or disruption.
36. Delegates work.
37. Transfers to employees the necessary authority for them to accomplish tasks.
38. Gives assignments to employees according to their strengths, weaknesses, and potential for personal growth.
39. Allows employees to complete assignments with support, but not interference.
40. Allows decisions to be made at the lowest appropriate level of his or her unit.
41. Considers employees' opinions in making decisions that affect their work.
42. Encourages employees to participate in the decision-making process in areas in which they believe they can contribute.
43. Explains his or her rationale for decisions with which employees disagree.
44. Manages decision making in a way that maximizes employees' commitment.

Norman Deets and Dr. Richard Morano, "Xerox's Strategy for Changing Management Styles," *Management Review Special Reports* (undated).

Span of Control: The More the Merrier?

Managers in restructured and downsized organizations suddenly find themselves with more people reporting to them. And yet, they are told, they must do more coaching. Therein lies a problem.

Mobil Oil's Elizabeth Julia Cole stresses the importance of the coaching role:

> At Mobil, we are redefining the manager's role. We want managers to manage and develop people, not just tasks. This is the bottom line: They have responsibility for developing to the highest potential each member of their staff, with strong commitment to teamwork rather than individual contributors.

Yet, when managers have more people reporting to them, where do they find the time to do coaching and development? Teresa McCaslin, vice president of human resources for Avery, believes part of the problem is the way managers approach their jobs.

> Many managers are too much into the details of the people who report to them. They're not focusing on their real role, which is to manage others, but not their *actual work*. It's hard for managers to pull out from day-to-day operations, but when they concentrate on details they don't have time for developing their people. And if you don't develop your people, then obviously you're not managing. It is the manager's role to be more of a resource than a director.

Managers who do their subordinates' work for them are actually *robbing them of the development they need*. This creates a vicious cycle, because subordinates continue to be dependent and are unable to take on added responsibility and decision-making authority. As a result, the managers must continue to be heavily involved in operational details and thus have no time for development and coaching—a classic case of co-dependency, because the managers become unhealthily dependent upon the dependency of their people on *them*.

GE's Jack Welch believes that a larger span of control is healthy because it puts more pressure on managers to allow their people to develop. He told *Harvard Business Review:*

> Remember the theory that a manager should have no more than six or seven direct reports? I say the right number is closer to 10 or 15. This way you have no choice but to let people flex their muscles, let them grow and mature. With 10 or 15 reports, a leader can focus only on big important issues, not on trivia.

Some middle managers would agree with Welch's view. One said:

> Span of control will be broadened and the challenges to be faced will be more complex. Unless the manager wants to spend his or her time putting out fires and doing the work, he or she must have a group of people who understand their roles, the tasks and philosophy of the organization, and are willing and able to act independently to help reach the common goal. If a manager insists on controlling every act and function of the group, it will slow down the company's ability to be flexible and fast-moving—thus making it less competitive. In the long run, no company can afford a manager who does not understand this.

One way to attack the problem of expanded span of control, says management consultant and author Allan Cox, is to develop decentralized teams of subordinates. "When management layers are eliminated, replace the management vacuum with teams of five to nine lower-level subordinates headed by a team leader," he recommends. "The leaders have authority to settle disagreements. Their responsibility is to achieve consensus and communicate it to higher management."

The End of Clonism: Managing a Diverse Work Force

Honeywell, Inc.'s Barbara Jerich has a corporate title that would have been unheard of 10 years ago: *director of work force diversity*. She says, "Before, we made people fit into a corporate mold filled with majority white male incumbents; now the corporations are going to have to change."

Why they will have to change is made abundantly clear by statistics on the demographic makeup of the U.S. work force that will emerge as we approach the 21st century. As of 1988, the U.S. work force was still dominated by white men. According to the Bureau of Labor Statistics, white males were 43 percent of the work force; white women were 36 percent; minority women, 11 percent; and minority men 10 percent. But more women and minorities are entering the work force than white men. Between 1988 and 2000, the entry rate will be 32 percent for white men, 35 percent for white women, 17 percent for minority women, and 16 percent for minority men. At the same time, far more white men—48 percent—will be *leaving* the work force. This compares with 35 percent for white women, 8 percent for minority women, and 9 percent for minority men.

The bottom line: women and minorities *will make up 85 percent of the net increase in the work force.* In the year 2000 the work force will be comprised of 38 percent white men, 36 percent white women, 13 percent minority women, and 13 percent minority men.

Small wonder, then, that many U.S. companies are beginning to address the problems that come with the increasing diversity of the work force.

For many of today's managers (who are still mostly white males) managing a diverse work force is another new role—and an uncomfortable one at that. Traditionally, managers have hired people in their own image. However unconsciously, they look hopefully for fraternity or college rings, service club insignia, or old school ties. They are curious about where the applicant lives, what the applicant's leisure activities are, what restaurants the applicant goes to. The whole idea is to identify the applicant as "my kind."

There are three major things wrong with this approach.

1. It is unlawful discrimination, since these criteria are not at all job related and tend to screen out minority and female candidates.
2. It deprives the organization of capable employees who are rejected simply because they don't fit the mold.
3. It is rapidly becoming impractical because of the increasing diversity of the work force shown by demographic statistics.

The Reagan years saw some backsliding on corporate affirmative action efforts. Recent Supreme Court decisions weakening long-established legal precedents in the civil rights area also contributed to the slippage (although at this writing, Congress seems about to pass legislation intended to nullify the effects of these decisions).

Now, however, many corporations are waking up to the fact that regardless of the climate in Washington, they have no choice but to hire and promote minorities and women for a very practical reason: nonwhites, women, and immigrants will make up more than five sixths of the net additions to the work force between now and 2000.

That makes managing diversity a strategic, bottom-line priority. And it means that managers must be guided and trained in the ability to evaluate, develop, and communicate with employees very different from themselves. It's not an ability that comes naturally, and many barriers must be overcome, including:

- Stereotypes and assumptions about people who are "different."
- Cultural differences that can make communication difficult.
- Unwritten rules and double standards that work against minorities and women.

- The "glass ceiling" that prevents minorities and women from being promoted beyond a certain level.
- The "white male club" syndrome.

Companies that have been wrestling with the problem of managing diversity for years provide some useful guidelines:

1. *Recognize the problem.* In too many organizations, top management simply fails to make the connection between managing work force diversity and organizational productivity and profitability. Until it does, it will ignore the problem or delegate and forget it, when management should be making an active commitment to the development of positive, innovative programs to address the problem.

2. *Talk about it.* Managers must confront and discuss their feelings about diversity in the work force. Back in the mid-1970s, Digital Equipment Company became aware of an unwritten rule that nobody talked about issues involving women and minorities—the subject was simply buried under the rug. The company then started a comprehensive program that enabled managers to talk openly and frankly about their feelings about working with people who were different from themselves. The program eventually evolved into a development process that helped managers to explore and identify group differences, strip away stereotypes, learn to listen and probe for differences in people's assumptions, and build relationships with people who are "different."

3. *Make managers accountable.* Aetna Life & Casualty in Hartford, Connecticut, has made selecting and managing a diverse work force a key measure on which middle managers are judged. The company holds workshops to deal with unstated assumptions about different groups of workers, and it has produced a television show dramatizing the issues involved. Some managers resisted the program at first, calling it fuzzy-headed and soft-hearted. But they

soon changed their minds when it was presented to them as a business issue.

Getting to Know You: The Need for Cross-Functional Collaboration

Cross-functional collaboration is a key skill today's manager must learn in order to function effectively in the new, more fluid organization. In solving problems, the manager must take many different perspectives into account rather than develop simplistic, narrow answers. For an organization to move fast—which it must to keep ahead of the competition—requires superb synchronization among departments. Many U.S. companies are far too compartmentalized, and the different parts of the organization don't speak to each other. A typical example comes from an industrial-products manufacturer. As the director of sales described it:

> We had downsized our sales and marketing departments, so we were faced with the problem of making them function more effectively with fewer people. Before the downsizing, the marketing department put a financial plan together, while at the same time the sales department was planning how much it would sell to every account. The two sets of numbers had never been put together. We asked ourselves, "If you don't put those numbers together, what good are they?" Now the marketing and sales goals are planned together by the two departments. By developing the joint numbers for next year by October, we were in good shape to allocate national sales goals and divide them up by regions and districts before the end of the year.

Welch's, the juice company, faced similar problems but found a way to solve them through restructuring. According to Jim Ryan, director of human resources:

> Historically, we had very strict departmental or functional compartmentalization. The different departments very rarely exchanged useful information except when problems arose. They rarely sat down with each other and discussed how one function might be able to interact and help another function.

One approach we used to solve this was to consolidate some operations under one officer. For example, manufacturing, quality assurance, logistics, and engineering now all report to the same officer. This has introduced new roles for managers, because it opened up lines of communication that were closed. Now our managers are learning to be total business contributors and to share their expertise with people outside their departments.

Because managers will increasingly be dealing with people outside their departments—people over whom they have no authority—the art of negotiation will be crucially important. Managers will have to recognize that there is more than one side to an issue and be ready to compromise, rather than stubbornly seek a win-lose victory. One's position, title, and authority will be less and less important as a means of getting things done through other people.

Today's manager must also deal with the growing fluidity of the modern organization. Traditional organizational models no longer work. David P. Norton, president of Nolan, Norton, & Company, explains why:

> Technology created the early organization form—an industrial, assembly-line technology—and then developed a structure that was consistent with it.... People couldn't interact with immediacy, so we had to create structures based on general assumptions. You designed a product, sent it to be manufactured, sold it, and there was always a set of stable relationships between the departments. These predictable, stable environments allowed us to create large-scale organizations. But now, massive organizations are seeking models for smaller entities within their frameworks. The industrial model is breaking down because we have a new technology that allows new relationships, new ways to react in organizations. That's at the heart of this transition away from an industrial era into a knowledge- or information-based era.
>
> The model "management by task force" involves uniting people with the skills required to solve a problem. An organization that forms executive-level task forces is managing according to objectives and processes that cut across traditional organizational boundaries.

Task forces that cross functional lines will be increasingly used in today's corporations. But middle managers need help in making the transition to this new way of working. One of the leading innovators in using the task force approach is Ford Motor Company. To bring its middle managers wholeheartedly into this radically new approach, Ford has instituted a program called LEAD. In *Fortune* magazine, Walter Kiechel III describes how it works:

> In the course of the 5½-day session that kicks off the program, managers are grouped by their functional specialties— manufacturing, finance, and so on—and asked to think about how their function works within the company, how others perceive it, and how it ought to work.
>
> But it's only when they discuss their conclusions with their colleagues from other functions that they really begin to find out how they're coming across: as quant jocks who only care about everybody else making their numbers, for example, or as stick-in-the-muds who routinely reject new approaches. "One group after another gets their brains beaten out," reports Michigan professor Robert Quinn, who helped design the program. "At the end of the week, one of the things they talk about most is the importance of cross-functional learning." Ford has a nice term for the process of getting people to think beyond their discipline: chimney-breaking.

Learning to Be a Rocket Scientist

In the past, managers were supposed to be good at the classic management tasks of planning, coordinating, directing, implementing, and control. Now, in addition to possessing those skills—and learning *not* to control when it is counterproductive—they are being asked to be wizards of innovativeness, creativity, and flexibility.

Increasing demands push many managers into uncharted waters where they are likely to flounder unless they are helped to achieve competence in these skills. But there's a big two-way payoff for doing so. The organization benefits because managers will be better able to carry out strategic goals under fast-moving, ever-changing conditions. Managers benefit from an opportunity to build their skills portfolios, thus making them eligible for more challenging and responsible jobs. Thus, developing skills represents an important way to help build a new partnership between the employer and the manager.

Turning on a Dime: The Art of Being Flexible
Flexibility was never a top priority for managers in rigidly institutionalized organizations where the environment was comfortably stable. Now it's a whole new ball game—one whose rules can change in mid-inning. Organizations are becoming more fluid in their structure as they try to meet the demand for faster product development and decision making. In the future, says Hudson Institute's William Johnson, companies will become "increasingly unstable collections of people."

A manager still needs to plan, but today's manager must learn to plan while running. There are no fixed points or predictable outcomes. Flexibility has moved to the forefront of managerial requirements.

Psychologist Harrison G. Gough defines flexibility as "the ability to shift and to adapt, to deal with the new, the unexpected, and unforeseen." However it is defined, achieving it may be difficult for many managers because they must unfreeze behaviors into which they have been locked for years. They may have gotten by in the past on the ability to solve routine business problems with routine solutions. That's no longer sufficient. Few problems are routine any more—and the ones that are usually don't require the manager's attention.

Flexibility means not only coming up with innovative solutions to unexpected problems, but also being receptive to those suggested by subordinates or peers (somehow it's less of a problem being receptive to those suggested by superiors).

Flexibility also means the ability to constantly work with different people in the organization. Gone are the days when a manager arrived in the morning to see the same old familiar faces day after day. During the course of one year, today's manager may be involved with four or five different task forces composed of people he or she has never worked with before. "We are moving toward a fluid system that clearly includes the concept of transience or temporary linkage," says futurist Alvin Toffler.

Encouraging Innovation

Helping managers become more flexible and innovative can have a salutary effect on their job performance. For example, managers who have been bogged down in deadly routine for many years tend to stagnate. They may operate on automatic pilot during the day and devote most of their enthusiasm and creative energies to interests outside their job. One way to revive their job enthusiasm and reengage their mental energies is to present them with new challenges. This can result in a far greater contribution to achieving company goals.

To bring about these results, however, requires that management foster and nurture a successful transition from rigidity and conformance to flexibility and creativity. How can it do that?

- Encourage a healthy attitude toward risk taking and the possibility of failure (the risk of failure is a vital ingredient of progress and development).
- When managers come up with innovative ideas and solutions, provide them with the resources to carry them out—or at least fully explore their value.
- Foster a climate that encourages creativity and innovation.
- Provide seminars in creative problem solving that will help managers develop the skills they need.
- Work individually with managers who may need special training in becoming more flexible and creative.

- Get managers into task-force situations where they will have the stimulus of other minds in developing innovative ideas and solutions.
- Give recognition to innovative ideas—*even when the ideas may not be practical.* After all, the idea is to encourage innovation, not to kill it.
- Give praise and publicity to successful groups, not just to individuals.

A MAJOR STEP TOWARD PARTNERSHIP

Helping managers learn new organizational roles can achieve two key goals. First, it will enable them to deliver the kind of performance that is so vitally needed for the organization to meet the competitive challenges ahead. Second, it will convey to managers that they are important participants in the formulation and implementation of their company's strategy. This can go a long way toward establishing a new partnership. But there is still much more to be done.

CHAPTER 8

THE PLATEAUED MANAGER: IS UP THE ONLY WAY TO GO?

One way to reduce the trust gap is to reduce the trust crap. The old "loyalty" is gone; it can't be brought back. Today's middle managers would rather deal with honest words from management about the realities of corporate life than phony baloney about loyalty. But that doesn't mean that you can't develop respect and trust between middle managers and their companies. It just has to be on a different basis.
—Middle manager in a large appliance firm

As we head into the 1990s, employers that want to attract and retain good managers should heed these words. Managerial talent is destined to become scarcer. David L. Birch, president of Cognetics, Inc., and author of *Job Creation in America: 1985–1995*, predicts that during the 1990s college-educated employees will be virtually able to name their own employment terms. And Princeton University sociologist Marvin Bressler observes: "For years, employers treated employees like commodities. Now employees can treat companies like commodities." And many will.

The post–baby boomers are not into permanence. Dr. Birch believes that, on average, students leaving college in 1990 can be expected to have some 10 or 12 jobs across three to five career fields. After being exposed to a few corporate jobs, they may take off on their own to establish firms themselves. "This is bad news for companies that need career people to manage the business," he says. "There will be few of these available. Graduates will fill entry-level positions all right, but most of them will be using the corporate job as a springboard into their postcorporate aspirations. The real corporate challenge will be keeping them on the payroll for more than five years."

Keeping good people is an increasingly critical issue as we head toward the next century. As U.S. corporations continue to dump their older managers—either through dismissal or early retirement—they will be more dependent on the younger generation of managers. According to the Bureau of Labor Statistics, one third of the men in this country between the ages of 55 and 64 have left the work force—almost double the proportion that left in 1970.

Many of the older managers who remain are disillusioned and distrustful. They are working not for the good of the company but solely for economic reasons: They have children in college, mortgage payments, parent-care expenses, and other financial obligations.

This does not bode well for the future competitiveness of U.S. corporations. Companies with managers who merely go through the motions may survive for a while, but eventually they will wither and die. Those companies that want to thrive, to increase market share and profitability, must attract and *retain* the best available managerial talent. And they can do that only by giving managers good reasons to contribute wholeheartedly to helping achieve company goals.

Creating a new kind of partnership, of course, requires the mutual efforts of both sides. This chapter deals with the efforts that it will be essential for corporate leaders to make. Only they can begin to forge a new relationship. After all, the tidal wave of downsizing and restructuring that has swept away so many middle managers was not their doing. In Chapter 9, we will discuss how middle managers can contribute to developing a new partnership.

IS A PARTNERSHIP POSSIBLE?

Is it naive to think that a partnership between middle managers and their companies can actually be achieved? Some would say, "You're damned right it is—true partners must be equal, and there's no equality between the two parties involved."

Legalistically that may be correct. However, we are not talking about a legal partnership. By *partnership,* we mean a relationship that involves close cooperation between two parties, each of whom has specific rights and responsibilities. These rights and responsibilities cannot be fully spelled out in written contracts. Instead, they must be based on mutual trust, on a belief by each party that the other will abide by the commitments it makes. And that is why, before any partnership can be established, the trust gap between managers and their companies must be closed.

Unfortunately, not many managements buy this concept. Organizational psychologist Kate Ludeman writes that few top executives see any connection between productivity and building trust and self-worth in their employees. Executives are often unwilling to change their fundamental attitudes toward employees and admit that "fuzzy" concepts such as integrity, willingness to share power, and ability to praise others have anything to do with how well or how hard people work.

On the other hand, says Ludeman, there are managers who dedicate themselves to building up the self-worth of their employees. They tell the truth, share power, praise good performance, and take practical action to show they care about their employees. They eschew political maneuvering and self-aggrandizement in favor of honest communication and genuine support for risk, innovation, and growth.

A FRESH UNDERSTANDING

Not all was right in the much-longed-for good old days. Indeed, the old parental relationship between managers and their companies was seriously out of balance. It resembled the military model: Soldiers obeyed orders without question and in return were fed, clothed, and housed. Similarly, employers secured organizational fealty from their middle managers with the inducements of security, raises, and promotions. Rewards were based chiefly on tenure, thus tying the fate of the organization closely to the fate of the middle manager. A manager might say, "OK, I'm going to do a great job with this company because its future is linked with mine—I'll be here for years and they're going to take care of me with steady promotions and raises, so I have a vested interest in doing everything I can to help this company achieve success."

Obviously, these are no longer the ties that bind, because they don't exist. Blind loyalty to the organization is a thing of the past. But that doesn't mean there is no hope for loyalty in the future. The new loyalty, however, will not necessarily be to the company. It will more likely be to the job, the profession, the project, the team, and the family. Ultimately, the most strongly felt loyalty of managers will be to themselves.

All this means there must be a greater equity in the new relationship between middle managers and their companies. Employers must now give far more attention to balancing and matching employee needs, goals, and capabilities with the organization's needs, goals, and requirements so that *both* can prosper.

This is a daunting challenge, because it means giving up long-accepted concepts of standard treatment for everyone. Middle managers (or any employees) can no longer be treated like interchangeable parts. Each individual has different needs and goals, and the diversity of these needs and goals will increase sharply with the growing diversity of the work force. Flexibility will be the key to building a high-morale, high-performance team of middle managers.

OUT WITH THE OLD, IN WITH THE NEW

When we talk about building a new partnership, the emphasis is on the word *new*. There's no going back—the terms of the old unwritten contract have been rendered null and void by profound changes in the global business environment. Since companies can no longer offer the inducements of the past to attract and retain managerial talent, they must find others. As the old Mau Mau saying goes: "If you take away something that a persons holds of value, you'd better be prepared to replace it with something of equal value." And to a more critical managerial work force, equal may not suffice.

To Keep Star Performers: Forget the Rule Book

Management consultant and author Michael J. Kami maintains that exceptional performers are entitled to exceptional treatment—even if it means departing from standard procedures. He cites one situation in which a manager was offered a cash bonus for outstanding work. But the manager didn't want his bonus in the form of money because he knew that when he brought the check home his wife would propose spending it on something he didn't particularly want, like a car. "Instead of money, give me a trip to Europe," he suggested to his boss. "The airline tickets, hotel reservations, traveler's checks." That way, he could go home and say, "Honey, we're going to Europe," and there wouldn't be a thing she could do about it.

It made sense to his boss, since it wouldn't cost the company any more. But the personnel vice president raised all kinds of objections: It would set a precedent, *everyone* would want an exception, and the company wasn't in the travel business. The manager's boss had to pound the desk to get what he wanted. But it was worth it—the manager continued to be phenomenally productive.

Here are the clauses in the old contract that must be replaced:

Old Clause: You'll keep your job as long as you perform reasonably well.

New Clause: We can't guarantee you a job forever—or even for five years. But as long as you're with us, we will invest in you just as we invest in our other key assets. And in investing in you, we will consult with you about the nature of our investment.

Old Clause: If you perform well, you will receive steady upward promotions and salary increases.

New Clause: We can't promise you steady promotions or salary increases—but we will provide appropriate rewards for outstanding performance in the form of monetary compensation (including equity, where possible), challenging work, and recognition. Moreover, we will fully explain our compensation policies and from time to time consult with you and your peers on improving our pay policies and procedures.

Old Clause: We'll plan your development to fit the approved career paths in our organization.

New Clause: We will not predetermine a traditional career path for you—but we will offer a variety of ways for you to progress and succeed. We expect you to control your own destiny by taking responsibility for your life and career planning, but we will do our best to help you grow toward your goals. Indeed, we will seek your advice about your own career path and the suitability of our company's other career paths.

Old Clause: We'll take good care of you so you don't have to worry about things like health care and retirement.

New Clause: We may not be able to provide all the benefits we provided in the past—but we will offer "customized" benefits. While the extent of these benefits will depend upon our ability to pay for them, their shape will be influenced by your needs.

Old Clause: If you stay the course for 25 years, you'll get a pin—maybe even a gold watch.

New Clause: We will try to build a relationship with you of trust and confidence by doing all of the above— and, *in addition,* we will communicate with you honestly and openly, share with you the information you need to help us meet our goals, and give you the freedom to take chances without fear of punishment for failure. We will, moreover, provide exceptional rewards for exceptional success. If you stay with us until you retire, we will provide you with appropriate affordable benefits—to the extent we can.

BRINGING THE NEW CONTRACT TO LIFE

Is Up the Only Way to Go?

Plateauing is now a fact of life for middle managers. There simply aren't the jobs to be promoted to any more—they've disappeared in the downsizing and restructuring frenzy of the 1980s. Look at General Electric, which once had 29 levels of management, from the CEO down to the mailroom supervisor. Now it has nine.

While many rungs on the corporate ladder have been eliminated, there are more and more baby boomers grasping for those that remain. A vital question for management is what to do about this disparity. Unless management comes up with some answers, it will have a disgruntled, frustrated middle-management work force on its hands just when it needs one that is fired up with enthusiasm.

The answer, of course, is not to put all those rungs back in place by adding layers of management. That might placate plateaued managers, but it would also make corporations unwieldy and slow-moving again. Instead, the answer must be found in alternative work motivators that do not depend on the carrot of promotion. And conversely, the scarcity of managerial talent makes the stick of fear a poor motivator as well.

Since the manager can no longer look at a job as simply a stepping-stone to a higher job, employers must increase the intrinsic worth of the manager's current job or of another job on the same level. This increased worth must be of enhanced value to both the manager and the employer.

Only a handful of companies are seriously attacking this problem. Their approaches are well worth consideration by any organization facing the probability of mass dissatisfaction in middle-management ranks.

Change Traditional Perceptions of Plateauing

"We've grown up in a culture where up was the way to go," points out Cheryl Smith, director of career management at Pacific Gas and Electric (P.G.& E.) in San Francisco. "We're trying to tell people what plateauing is, what it is not, and that it's okay. We're saying, 'Wait a minute, wait a minute. It's okay to move laterally.' "

The virtues of moving sideways instead of up may not be immediately apparent to a middle manager conditioned to believe that progress is synonomous with promotions. Nevertheless, lateral mobility *can* be an effective way to further personal growth, career development, and job satisfaction. It can give managers an opportunity to get out of jobs in which they have been stagnating and into jobs that provide new stimulation and fresh challenges. And the organization can end up having managers with more rounded capabilities, diversified skills, and renewed enthusiasm.

One of middle managers' greatest misgivings about being plateaued is that it signifies personal failure. P.G.&E. tackles this perception problem with educational efforts to persuade employees that plateauing carries no stigma but is simply an organizational reality. Lectures by consultant psychologists and articles in company newsletters also make this point to P.G.&E. employees.

Eastman Kodak's career development plan stresses that career development does not imply upward movement, but rather "lifelong learning and growth." Says Cindy M. Cahill, retraining manager in the Kodak Park Division, "We convey to our employees that career development is a process that applies to everyone and is more than just 'movement up the ladder.'"

Provide More Psychological Ownership of the Job

The more autonomy an employee gets, the less likely he or she is to feel like a "cog in the wheel." Says Stanley Tilton, president of Right Associates:

> The manager who wants to be in a higher job immediately devalues his or her present job. You must give managers more ownership to the job so they can be more creative in developing the different skills and knowledge that lead to growth. Giving managers more autonomy enables them to take more responsibility for what the job should be, rather than just going by the job description, which was probably written five years ago and is obsolete.

More autonomy is a mixed blessing for some managers, because it means they must put more time and effort into making decisions and negotiating for resources. Some managers actually prefer a more traditional arrangement: the boss calls and says, "I want that report on my desk by Thursday morning." Not enjoyable, but fast and clear-cut.

Despite this reservation, strong evidence exists that having more autonomy creates greater job enthusiasm in the majority of managers. For example, a survey of 325 middle and upper-middle managers by Dunhill Personnel System, Inc., shows that 59 percent derived more job satisfaction because they were given greater control over their jobs—despite the fact that they were also working harder and putting in longer hours. Commenting on this finding, Joel Brockner, associate professor at Columbia Graduate School of Business, said: "These managers have developed a stronger sense of autonomy. They may be feeling more stress because of longer hours and heavier work loads, but they are happier with the challenges and greater responsibilities that their jobs provide."

Companies that are restructuring have a two fold interest in giving their middle managers more say. One is that as these companies get rid of entire layers of management, each remaining manager's span of control increases and less supervision is possible. This necessitates autonomy of action and individual decision making. Second, this autonomy generates a higher level of commitment and ownership in the middle-management group.

But giving managers more autonomy can backfire unless they are also given training and coaching so they can successfully handle their new decision-making freedom. Otherwise, there won't be job satisfaction—but there will be stress, failure, and burnout.

Help Middle Managers Grow within Their Jobs

Promotions, of course, create a significant opportunity for growth. But with promotions so scarce, their role in stimulating development and growth will diminish sharply. Now the bulk of growth opportunities must be found—and created— either within the job itself or in lateral moves to other jobs.

A 1988 survey by Wick and Company, a research and consulting firm based in Wilmington, Delaware, suggests that companies whose career-development strategies rely mainly on promotions will not maximize the contributions of their managers. On the contrary, meaningful development is greater when companies create growth opportunities with assignments on the manager's current job. The survey included more than 600 managers and professionals in eight Fortune 500 companies.

The survey showed that tasks and relationships occurring *within* assignments accounted for 44 percent of all key developmental experiences, while promotions accounted for

11 percent. (The remaining growth experiences were derived from training, nonpromotional job change, and various other experiences both on and off the job.)

The respondents defined these experiences as value-added opportunities: real problems whose solutions added value to the organization. These included:

- Participation in task teams.
- Being assigned to special projects.
- Filling in for a supervisor.
- Handling a crisis.
- Creating a new system, product, or approach.

All of these experiences had one thing in common: The manager had to confront an unfamiliar problem that involved the risk of failure. A typical experience was that of an insurance company manager:

> When our company agreed to write a new insurance plan, it caused a large sudden growth in activity for our office. This caused me to have to create a unit to handle just these claims. I was given authority to hire staff and assign responsibility to the various units. This was an exciting time . . . and won us applause from everyone. I learned to utilize the department for more responsive claims service. I found that people could be encouraged to work as a team. I found how necessary it was for the manager to constantly build enthusiasm and morale.

Provide Opportunities for Short-Term Accomplishment

Many middle managers complain that they never see the results of their work—or if they do, the results are a long way down the road. A feeling of accomplishment in their jobs is missing. That feeling becomes an increasingly important motivator as the chances of climbing up the hierarchical ladder fade. Being able to say, "I had a part in doing that," is a major source of job satisfaction and stimulates enthusiasm for the jobs ahead.

Robert H. Schaffer, author of *The Breakthrough Strategy: Using Short-Term Successes to Build the High Performance Organization,* points out that the same powerful forces that stimulate performance surges in a crisis can be replicated in short-term projects aimed at producing immediate, measurable performance results.

Short-term projects cannot only provide excitement, challenge, and satisfaction for participating employees. They can also make companies more competitive by helping to improve the processes by which they design, develop, produce, and market their goods and services.

A striking example is provided by Ingersoll-Rand—not an entrepreneurial, go-go upstart, but a $3 billion machinery and equipment company founded in 1871. Ingersoll faced a critical challenge. It was taking longer and longer for the company to design and make a product, while its Pacific Rim competitors were speeding up the process. In 1987 Ingersoll's product-development cycle was getting close to four years. Then the company formed a task force—called the Strykeforce after its leader, James D. Stryker. The team's mission: to turn out a new portable air grinder in *one year.*

To meet that goal, the team abandoned the traditional, linear product-development process, in which marketing thought up a product, handed it to engineering, which designed it and passed it to manufacturing, which made it and presented it to sales. The system was slow, cumbersome, frustrating.

In its place, Stryker formed a cross-functional team made up of sales, marketing, engineering, and manufacturing people working together. As one team member put it: "Everyone would play in the same sandbox. We were going to share our pails and shovels."

One year later, the new grinder was presented to Ingersoll distributors. It had been a year filled with obstacles, crises, and some serious dissension. But it was also a year in which all members of the team felt they had a stake in every step of the process. And in the end they had not only the satisfaction of meeting their goal, but also of developing a process that could speed up the development of many other Ingersoll products.

Provide Recognition for Accomplishments

When a company well known for its enlightened management practices conducted an internal employee opinion survey, it found some of the results deeply disturbing. In one question, employees were asked to indicate their level of agreement or disagreement with the statement: "I get recognition from management when I do my job well." Although there was improvement over the previous survey two years before, a surprisingly large number of employees reported they were *not* receiving appropriate recognition. Some of the anonymous comments were:

> "I know I do my job well, but it would be nice to be told this once in a while."
>
> "Never a thank you, and rarely any praise. But I do get *complaints* when something goes wrong."
>
> "My work is just taken for granted. There is a total lack of recognition."

This survey's results were consistent with the responses of employees in other organizations that take employee opinion polls. The unavoidable conclusion is that vast numbers of men and women in the U.S. work force feel unpraised, unrecognized, even unacknowledged for their efforts.

Eighteenth-century poet Edward Young wrote, "The love of praise, howe'er concealed by art, reigns more or less, and glows in ev'ry heart." But who needs a poet to tell us that we need praise? All of us know that most human beings want recognition and, indeed, honest praise for work well done. Yet lack of recognition and praise was one of the major complaints we heard in our interviews with managers.

Why management fails so miserably at this is baffling. How much time does it take to thank someone, to make a quick phone call, or to scribble a note? How much does such a gesture cost? How much is such a gesture *worth?* From a cost/benefit standpoint, what could be more effective than an encouraging word or a well-timed smile? Why don't we do it? What costs in demotivated employees do we incur by neglecting this fundamental human act?

What Would Motivate Me: Managers Speak Out

We asked middle managers to tell us what would restore their enthusiasm for their jobs. Here's a sampling of their answers:

- What would it take to rejuvenate my lost dedication to my employer? First, a belief that the mission of the company is to provide a needed product or service, not short-run maximum stockholder return at any cost. Second, a belief that the company understands that an organization is driven by people, is customer oriented, and is honest.

- I have often considered why I would stay and what would make me go. Steady promotions are a thing of the past, but job enrichment and expansion are distinct inducements. Even if I'm trapped in a middle-management role, I would like the opportunity to accept more job responsibility and expand my horizons. The culture of the corporation and how I fit in is one of the most important facts for me. When it comes to compensation, incentive bonus plans are attractive, and earlier vestment in retirement plans is another draw card. An equity position would also help in a publicly owned corporation, as long as it is a meaningful share.

- In restoring trust, honesty is the key word. It is the foundation of trust in any relationship. We all know there are good times and there are bad, but management should honestly communicate where we stand at any given moment.

- What are the three things that motivate me to do a good job?

  1. A cooperative environment in which conflicts can be resolved through compromise or trade-offs. We're the first generation that expects the work place to be fun. We don't like to go to a job where everyone is snarling at each other all day.

What Would Motivate Me (continued)

2. Recognition for a job well done. I know of few people who don't feel better after getting praise for a job well done. I'm not saying we should be receiving daily strokes for the job we are expected to do, but on occasions of extra effort it is deserved.

3. The freedom to control my department. I want to be trusted to do my best with the projects and guidelines that come down to me. I like to see my ideas go directly to the top with very little editing. This is a satisfaction that makes me want to do my best on the next assignment that comes along.

- I want goal setting to be a two-way process. If I'm working for you, and you say, okay, this year I want you to come up with ten new clients, and I think to myself, hey, the average is two a year and he wants me to get ten, that's unrealistic, it's not fair. So I say, well, how about four? And he says, okay, let's make it five.

- I want to work for a company that levels with me, that keeps me informed, that tries to include my thoughts and feelings in the overall management process. Dialogue is the key.

Broaden the Manager's Job Challenge

A narrow, restrictive managerial job can eventually dampen enthusiasm. This is an increasingly serious problem now that the manager knows that there's probably no escape through promotion to a job with more varied responsibilities. Some companies are helping their managers cross the boundaries of their own departments and deal with broader challenges.

One of these companies is Mass Mutual. The objective of its Professional Development Boards program is twofold: to stimulate cross-fertilization among its lines of business and to provide its managers with a larger perspective. CEO Tom Wheeler says:

Like a lot of good ideas, Professional Development Boards are not new—they originated with the McCormick Company many years ago. But we find that they definitely apply to the needs of today's organization. Basically, we bring members of different divisions, departments, and lines of business together in task forces or committees to focus on solving corporate problems, developing new initiatives, and exploring synergistic opportunities. They meet periodically, usually once a week. These are not senior managers—they are middle managers, supervisors, and associates.

Our Boards give them a chance to meet people from other units, and to understand the problems, the challenges, and the opportunities that exist in the corporation. We think our Boards are successful because they not only produce usable ideas, but the participants get a lot out of them. First, they feel that they're making a significant contribution. Second, they have a better understanding of the company. Third, there's a certain amount of prestige involved. So the whole process is really an experience in personal growth, and I think it stimulates a certain sense of loyalty based on the feeling that the company really is interested in giving them unique career options that might not be available otherwise. And they get a lot of satisfaction out of knowing that their ideas are being supported and utilized by the company (not in every instance, of course).

Ultimately, I believe, participation on the Boards *gives more meaning to the work they're doing.*

Base Compensation on Contributions, Not Hierarchy

Psychological motivators are just as important as monetary motivators, but one type cannot substitute for the other—you must have both to keep good people. As one middle manager said, "I like praise, but you can't put it in the bank." And this is a particularly sensitive issue when middle managers see senior executives raking in multimillion-dollar incomes. Middle managers don't expect their bosses to live in dire poverty, but they think CEOs get too big a slice of the pie.

Meaningful pay raises have traditionally been based on promotions to higher positions. No longer. In today's flatter organizations, there aren't enough promotions to go around.

For plateaued middle managers, other, innovative criteria must be found on which to base their rewards—or the best ones will leave.

What about merit increases? Theoretically they are based on performance and therefore should be an effective way of rewarding plateaued managers for their contribution. In practice, however, merit increases don't do what they are supposed to do: differentiate among various levels of performance.

Many middle managers consider merit increases to be a joke—on them. In an *Industry Week* readership survey on compensation, 76 percent of the responding managers did not believe that their companies genuinely granted increases based on merit. The reason: subjective biases of their appraisers. One manager said, "It all boils down to how well the boss likes you."

Another complaint by middle managers is that when it comes to handing out merit increases there is little differentiation between adequate performance and outstanding performance. According to a Hay Group study of industrial companies in 1988, an employee who received a "satisfactory" rating received an average 4.7 percent raise, while "outstanding" performers were given 7.7 percent. In terms of actual dollars, this means that a $40,000-a-year middle manager with a satisfactory rating would earn $27 more a week, while an outstanding $40,000-a-year manager would take home $44. Not exactly an incentive to put forth one's best efforts.

This is the result of applying a civil-service mentality to compensation administration. When this happens, raises are routine and predictable, and thus they become virtual entitlements in the minds of employees rather than incentives to do an outstanding job. In the federal government, merit increases are so automatic that one federal employee said, "In order not to get the raise, you have to hit your supervisor or not come to work."

You can say the same about many private-sector organizations. The narrow range of merit increases is usually mandated by company policy. Managers are told they cannot exceed an average of, let's say, 7 percent, when they hand out raises. Staying within this average makes it virtually impossible to give outstanding performers substantially higher increases than mediocre ones.

Middle Managers—No Slice of the Pie?   Companies that recognize this problem are beginning to shift away from traditional merit increase systems to what are known as variable pay plans. These plans enable management to take a much more flexible approach to compensating its middle managers and other employees. But so far, this trend has had only a limited impact on the middle-management level. Look at the results of a 1990 study by Towers Perrin:

- In companies with $500 million to $1 billion in sales, a mere 23 percent of middle managers in the $40,000–$50,000 range get variable pay.
- In companies with sales of more than $6 billion, only 11 percent of managers in this salary range receive variable pay.
- Of those who do get variable pay, most earn no more than 2 percent of their total income from it.

Towers Perrin made a similar study of midlevel managers and professionals earning $20,000 to $50,000 a year, showing that *only 1 percent* of their pay was tied to performance bonuses. Even nonmanagerial employees were being given gainsharing incentives that were not offered to middle managers, Towers Perrin says.

The news seems to be a bit brighter in smaller firms than larger ones. A 1989 survey by Hewitt Associates of companies with $10 million to $100 million in annual sales shows that for managers, gains in total cash compensation (base salary plus bonus) outpaced increases in base salary by a substantial margin. At the corporate level, for example, base pay increases averaged 4.6 percent, while increases in total compensation averaged 7.3 percent.

So middle managers view all the talk about incentive pay as mostly hype. Corporations offer several explanations of why they don't have more variable pay programs for the middle level, when they offer them to people above and below that level. They say that variable pay for middle managers is too expensive, while for nonmanagerial employees it is practically free because it is based on productivity gains. They point out that it is difficult to rate the performance of middle managers as a basis for incentive pay. Eastman Kodak, for example, dropped achievement of personal goals as a factor in determining bonus pay for middle managers because it was hard to quantify. Now the only factors used are corporate and divisional results.

Conspicuously absent from corporate explanations of the performance pay disparity is that once top executives have established their own bonuses, there's little left in the pot for middle managers. They also seem to ignore the fact that the performance of some top managers is probably even more difficult to measure than that of middle managers, and yet they get their yearly bonuses. Marc J. Wallace, Jr., business professor at the University of Kentucky, maintains that in many companies standards for top executive bonuses are adjusted to make it easy for them to get the bonuses they want.

For middle managers, variable pay programs have their pluses and minuses. One big drawback is that such programs put more of their income at risk. Income is not as predictable as it was when routine merit increases were the norm. And with certain types of compensation alternatives, income could actually go *down*.

Despite these disadvantages, most managers, faced with the prospect of being plateaued, see pay for performance as the only way they can substantially improve their income. A

1990 *Industry Week* survey of its readers showed that about two thirds would like to see their pay tied to performance, based on either the performance of the organization, performance of their operating unit, or performance measured by individual achievement of goals.

A group of eight middle managers extensively interviewed by Amanda Bennett for *The Wall Street Journal* were unanimous in preferring a compensation system based on rewards for team and individual performance that include extraordinary bonuses. They wanted to be paid more directly for their performance in meeting goals—and they believe their bosses should be paid similarly. Bennett quotes one customer-service manager for a large public utility that does that. "I feel pretty good about it," he said. "You all have shared goals. There's a different amount of risk in each package, so you really incent people to do exceptional work, and not reward people for just hanging on."

Pay for performance can benefit plateaued managers because it does an end run around a major obstacle to their being able to improve their income: pay based on hierarchy. In the past, when there were well-defined salary gaps between different levels of the organization, the only possible way you could boost your income beyond a certain top limit was to be promoted to a higher level. Now that this avenue has been closed to most middle managers, there are only two alternatives: pay based on contribution with less emphasis on level or leaving the company for another job with higher pay. This lays it out clearly for employers who want to hold on to their best managers: Either give them the opportunity to earn more money or get ready to wave them good-bye.

Properly designed and implemented, variable pay programs can produce a win-win outcome for middle managers and their companies. Companies can benefit from:

- Retaining their best managers.
- Stimulating higher performance levels in all their managers.

• Reducing fixed compensation costs.

The last item, of course, is a major motivator for companies that must be ever mindful of the cost crunch that is facing them during the 90s. As Walt Winder, vice president and compensation expert at Towers, Perrin, Forster & Crosby, points out: "Companies want to get away from entitlement compensation because all regular salary increases do is increase the base level of fixed costs. It's like an annuity. It goes on forever."

But this will be a false savings for companies whose only motivation is to cut down on their fixed compensation costs. Unless they design and implement variable pay programs that will actually motivate and satisfy their middle-management work force, they will find their savings more than offset by the results of low morale and poor productivity.

The Many Faces of Variable Pay. What is *variable pay?* Simply put, it is any kind of pay given strictly on the basis of employee or corporate performance. This differentiates it from pay given through standard salary increases. But within the variable pay category there are many approaches that can be used. Every company should evaluate the options carefully, because the wrong variable pay approach can do more harm than good. There is no point, for example, in basing rewards on team effort in an organization where the work is done primarily by individual contributors.

However, companies have a number of options in creating variable pay programs:

• *Special performance targets.* Basically, this is an upscale name for our old friend *piecework,* transplanted from the factory floor to the office. But for managers, rewards would be based not on individual contributions but on department performance.

• *Lump-sum merit.* Another fancy moniker for what could be more simply called a bonus—except that this payment replaces, rather than supplements, a salary increase. This approach helps companies to keep their compensation costs down because it's a one-shot deal. Rather than adding a merit increase to the manager's base salary, the company awards the increase at the end of the year in one cash payment, while the base salary remains unchanged. This is one of the most striking trends in compensation: traditional yearly increases in base salaries are losing out to lump-sum merit increases. An example is the system used by Betz Equipment Systems in Horsham, Pennsylvania. A manager with a base salary of $30,000 who does a good job the first year would get $33,000, but the base salary would remain the same. A better job the following year would earn the manager $34,500 with no increase in base salary. Only in the third year would actual salary be increased as a platform for future bonuses—and from then on an increase in base salary comes every three or four years.

• *Profit sharing.* Many companies tout profit sharing as an effective way to retain their best managers. Under this plan, rewards are tied to the company's overall yearly profit—if profits are up, a portion of the additional income is distributed throughout the company. Not all managers are enthusiastic about this approach. Profits can go down, as well as up—and often through no fault of the employees. There may be no connection between a manager's individual effort and what happens to profits. *Business Week* quoted one manager as saying: "Last year I got the biggest bonus I've ever gotten, and the money was nice. But it didn't make me feel good. Nothing I did affected my bonus because it's based on overall corporate earnings. Did I work any harder or less hard? No. The industry just went up." (He didn't return the check, however.)

• *Team incentives.* Probably one of the most promising forms of variable pay, even though it was used by only 18 percent of 501 companies surveyed by The Conference Board in 1989. Under this plan, awards are based on the performance of small groups rather than individuals or the whole corporation. This approach has two advantages: It ties rewards more closely to individual performance than profit sharing, but at the same time, it does not create the cutthroat competition and managerial jealousy that can be created by rewards based on individual contributions. But there are drawbacks as well. Friction can arise between high producers on the team and low producers who are dragging down the team's average performance. Still, over time an informal system of peer evaluation and peer pressure may give important messages to the poorer performers.

• *Skill-based pay.* Though it has been widely discussed, paying people for the skills they have rather than for the jobs they do is not an approach that has been much used for managers. This is typically applied in manufacturing plants—employees learn different skills in the production process and are rewarded for having these skills. In office environments, the acquisition of advanced word processing skills may bring higher compensation.

But why not apply skill-based pay to middle managers? This would seem to be a natural way to increase compensation for plateaued managers who have little chance of pay progression through promotion. As Edward E. Lawler III and Gerald E. Ledford, Jr., point out:

> One way to ameliorate this problem is to use a skill-based pay system under which employees are paid for horizontal as well as for vertical learning, and are given increases and opportunities to grow and develop. In this way, skill-based pay could be a partial solution to the problem of career satisfaction, and could serve to legitimize the idea that a good career move can be horizontal, not just vertical.

However, there are continuing debates about just what skills and competencies go to make an effective manager.

• *Stock options.* Compensation through stock options is nothing new but has until recently been limited to senior executives. In fact, quite a few of these top managers are making fortunes through their stock options. For example, Michael D. Eisner, Walt Disney Company chairman, collected a neat $32 million from exercising his stock options in 1988.

Now the use of stock options is spreading downward to include upper-middle managers. Pepsico—and earlier, Pfizer—have established stock-option programs for virtually *all* their employees. Still, this is the exception in corporate America.

Measuring Managerial Performance. Pay-for-performance programs put new pressure on management to find better ways of *measuring* performance. Pay for performance is meaningless unless it is based on valid criteria. And most managers don't believe that their performance is evaluated fairly and objectively. According to research by the Hay Group, says partner Peter Gelfond, politics is perceived by most managers as the basis for rewards.

A major problem is that appraisers are not given specific guidelines for rating their subordinates. Mobil Oil was mindful of this problem when it decided to develop a new compensation system based on performance. According to Mobil's Elizabeth Julia Cole:

> Our new appraisal form incorporates specific competencies that would be found in outstanding managers. We are more clearly defining what is job performance against particular job specifications. That way we are really and truly going to differentiate between those who perform at a high level and those at an adequate level. Not that people who perform adequately can't get increases. But our merit system before just did not allow significant differentiation between adequate performance and outstanding performance.
>
> We are more clearly defining competencies so that appraisers can be more accurate. In the past, we would simply list the competencies, such as "Effective communication." Now they are defined: "If somebody has this competency, they do such and such. If they don't, this is what you'll see." Our competencies for management positions include such qualities as encouraging teamwork, effective delegation, and improving the organization.

However, many managers—even those who are given more specific guidelines—typically find that conducting an appraisal interview is difficult and can be unpleasant. Who wants to get into an argument about whether an employee has ineffective communication skills, for example? Performance measures based on incontrovertible results may yield more accurate assessments than those based on skills.

Can a Plateaued Manager Be a Committed Manager?

The answer is yes—provided that the manager is given other incentives besides promotions that may never come. These incentives include:

- Psychological ownership of the job.
- Opportunities for growth in professional skills.
- Opportunities for short-term accomplishment.
- Recognition for work well done.
- Broad new job challenges that go beyond departmental boundaries.
- Lateral moves that can provide fresh stimulus.
- Compensation that genuinely reflects outstanding performance.

By providing these incentives, employers can go a long way toward establishing a new partnership with their managers. But both companies and their managers can make further contributions toward that goal.

CHAPTER 9

RESTORING TRUST: THE END OF "THEM VERSUS US"

There is an ancient English word, concinnity, *that means a skillful fitting together of parts; an elegant harmony. That's what we need to develop among the human beings who make up our business enterprises. Most employees want to work for the good of the company if there's a climate of mutual trust and respect. Mutual trust comes through an attitude of optimism about the worth of people. Developing and nurturing this attitude are major tasks of management today.*

It would be naive to believe that middle managers will ever see things exactly the way that top management does. Many middle managers will always tend to think in terms of "them" and "us." But does it have to be "them" *versus* "us"? Not if employers take steps to close the hierarchy gap that is pervasive throughout so many organizations. Management must make genuine, intensive efforts to reduce the wide difference in the perception of the organization between itself and its middle managers as part of the new contract.

BRINGING MIDDLE MANAGERS INTO THE LOOP

Giving middle managers a feeling of ownership can do much to close the perception gap. This can be done partially through financial means, such as employee stock option plans (ESOPS). But that won't necessarily bring middle managers closer to top management in terms of *trust*. That can only be done, says Mass Mutual CEO Tom Wheeler, by giving managers more freedom to speak up and to participate in solving organizational problems. He says:

> I think it is a matter of *bringing them into the loop* so that they feel they can speak their piece in an environment that promotes some risk taking. It means making them part of the solution rather than the problem. It means letting them know:
> 1. That you want their ideas and thoughts on getting things done.
> 2. That mistakes, while they cannot be tolerated *ad infinitum*, will be considered learning experiences.
> 3. That if a mistake occurs because somebody stretched, that doesn't mean 10 lashes and go to the end of the line. It means you tried it, it didn't work, but let's learn from it and move on.

Hay Group's Peter Gelfond sees a wall between top and middle management that prevents a better blending of perceptions about the organization. That wall, he believes, is created by senior managers just below the top echelon. In average organizations, he says, they are failing to make the middle managers below them part of the team.

Unfortunately, top management is usually too isolated from middle management to notice the problem. This is borne out by such data as the survey of chief executives of 164 large firms conducted in 1989 by A. Foster Higgins & Company, an employee-benefits consulting firm. Most of the CEOs agreed that personal communication helps to increase the commitment and job satisfaction of employees—*but 86 percent said that other demands on their time prevented them from doing enough communicating.*

One wonders if some of those "other demands" are not generated by problems arising from a lack of cohesion between themselves and their middle managers. If so, it is peculiarly short-sighted for company leaders to ignore the need for closer collaboration between the middle and the top. One former manager who experienced poor communication from the top in a large company—and has since started his own business—says: "It's tremendously important to keep your middle managers informed, to include their thoughts and feelings in the overall management process. And that means spending time to dialogue with them."

Confidentiality is the enemy of trust. Yet many top managements persist in believing that certain information is not for the ears of those below the highest level. One consultant reports that when he suggested to the CEO of a large company that it would be helpful to discuss management's overall strategy with middle managers, the chief executive replied: "You can't discuss this—it's our strategy, it's confidential, and it's for the senior executive group." Nor is this an isolated example. A 1989 survey by the General Accounting Office showed that only 45 percent of large, publicly held companies provide employees with information on business plans and goals.

Small wonder that most employees say they don't know what's going on at their companies—and that damaging rumors often fill the void.

Even some CEOs who do communicate with middle managers and other employees seem to think that *personal* communication is unnecessary. They send out memos, they publish messages in the house organ (usually written by the editor), they even make video presentations. Then they can't understand why their people aren't all fired up by the company vision.

The reason is that employees want to hear from a live person. They want to be able to ask questions and to contribute their own ideas. They want *responses*—which they're not going to get from a memo or a video screen.

Tom Nies, CEO and president of Cincom Systems, Inc., the world's largest privately held computer software company, believes that a top executive must be highly visible and accessible. "The CEO has to see and be seen by his employees," he says. "You can't run this business by the numbers and simply look at rating sheets. An active, physical presence is essential."

Dan R. Bannister, president and CEO of Dyncorp, an employee-owned company that provides technical and professional services to the commercial aviation industry and to U.S. and foreign government agencies, is heading up an effort to build a spirit of teamwork throughout his organization. One of the most important aspects of these efforts, he believes, is personal communication:

> Good internal communications is a top priority for our senior managers. They spend a large amount of time out in the field with employees—and we have 18,000 employees at about 150 sites throughout the world. We also hold employee annual meetings (just like stockholder meetings) at locations throughout the company. The only way to establish a teamwork climate in a company is for top management, including the CEO, to get out among the employees and talk about teamwork and demonstrate how it can work.

Unfortunately, leaders who don't practice this kind of personal communication usually aren't even aware that middle managers' perceptions of the organization differ drastically from their own. The reason is that just as downward communication—except for orders and imposed policies—is missing, so is upward communication. When lines of communication are clogged in both directions, there is no chance of one group understanding the other.

And yet there is a desperate need for two-way communication. Studies by the Hay Group show that employees want "reliable information on where the company is headed" and "how my job fits into the total."

Management guru W. Edwards Deming, who introduced management methods to Japan after World War II that are just now catching on in the United States, maintains that as many as four of every five managers would have difficulty describing their jobs with any precision. Yet in today's globally competitive environment, each manager (and every employee) needs to know with certainty his or her job and to understand the jobs of others upon whose results they depend. In too many organizations, however, employees and managers exist in a world of ambivalence and ambiguity. In such organizations, few employees understand the company's mission or its values.

Burson-Marsteller, a large and successful multinational public relations firm, presents a striking exception. The basic missions, goals, and beliefs of the agency have been articulated in a document called "Our Vision, Our Values." Meetings on this subject were held at the firm's branches all over the world at a cost of more than $1 million. All staff members were told that "high energy, hard work, even a high threshold of pain are constants at Burson-Marsteller," and that the qualities of achievement, teamwork, commitment, curiosity, sharing, and risk are encouraged. The document emphasizes that "We exist solely to serve our clients." Not much ambiguity there.

BOOSTING THE BELIEVABILITY QUOTIENT

Unclogging lines of communication between top management and middle management (both up and down) is only the first step in closing the hierarchy gap. Just any kind of communication is not going to increase top management's credibility in the eyes of already cynical middle managers. The communication must have a high believability quotient or it will fall on deaf ears.

All evidence, both anecdotal and formal, suggests that this is one of the most serious problems creating distrust of the top. For example, when Carnegie Mellon University Professor Robert Kelley surveyed 400 managers in 1990, he discovered that they didn't believe what top management said over half the time. They complained that top executives were not open with them and often misled them about what was actually happening in the organization.

How can top management play straight with its middle managers and other employees? Several guidelines come to mind:

• *Don't pretend that things are better than they are.* Expressing optimism is one thing, but misleading employees is another. They should be told candidly where the organization stands. Perhaps some will get out their résumés. But most will be more committed to solving the problems of the organization if they know that top management is telling them the truth. When top management withholds bad news, chances are that the communication vacuum will be filled by rumors that may be even worse than the reality.

• *Find out what middle managers are thinking—and give them a response.* Unfortunately, the companies most in need of employee feedback are the very ones who are least likely to seek it. Only 45 percent of large employers periodically conduct employee surveys, according to A. Foster Higgins & Co. Even the companies that do survey often don't share the results with the employees themselves. This simply reinforces employee beliefs that management doesn't really care what they think anyway.

Enlightened, high-performing companies, on the other hand, take frequent pulse readings of their middle managers and other employees. Then they respond to what they perceive as "red flags"—warnings that there are feelings out there that must be addressed.

Employees want feedback on the results. Says Peter Gelfond of the Hay Group, which does employee surveys for major companies:

> Employees what to know how they compare with others in their opinions and feelings about the organization. "Am I the only one who feels underpaid?" "Am I the only one who feels

there's a problem with my retirement plan?" They also realize that when their company feeds back results, it probably will consider and respond to these findings.

This doesn't mean that management can always say, "Yes, we will take care of that problem tomorrow." They may have to say, "We can deal with some of the problems you raise, but not others," and then explain fully why that is so. Assuming that the reasons are valid, employees will certainly prefer this to feeling that their responses have vanished into a deep, dark hole.

Gelfond reports that most Hay Group clients survey employees approximately every 18 months. However, they also want to get feedback between major surveys. For example, if a company has installed a new pay-for-performance program, it would like to know whether the impact is favorable. However, says Gelfond it is self-defeating to overburden employees with detailed surveys. Hay Group has devised one answer to that problem: a user-friendly telephone survey. Using a touch-tone telephone system, employees listen to a short questionnaire, perhaps 16 items on one or two topics. They respond to the multiple-choice questions by pushing numbered buttons. The whole thing takes a few minutes and employers can get their feedback within 24 hours.

In addition, there are other methods that companies can utilize to open up the communication lines between middle managers and top management. Meetings can be effective—*if* they make it possible for real communication to take place. Traditionally, meetings with middle managers are one-way affairs at which they are exhorted to give their all for the cause. And traditionally, these meetings get a ho-hum, we've-heard-it-all-before response. Managers get the feeling that *their* input is not wanted. And if they believe they have been used and abused, they will simply laugh grimly (and silently) at top management's assertions that they are the most important people on earth.

The Chow Still Stinks

The worst sin in conducting employee opinion surveys is failing to act on the results. In the *New York Times,* Claudia H. Deutsch tells of one manager who recalled an employee survey at his company that produced many complaints about the cafeteria. Although management reported the survey's results in the employee newsletter, it did nothing about the cafeteria complaints.

"Before, we could kid ourselves that the bosses did not know how bad the cafeteria was," the manager said. "After the survey, we knew they just didn't care."

Claudia H. Deutsch, "Asking Workers What They Think," *New York Times,* April 22, 1990.

To close the trust gap, any meeting between middle managers and top management must include *two-way* communication. Managers must be encouraged to speak frankly about their concerns—and top management must be willing to listen with open minds rather than taking the view that "These middle managers are always griping about something." It is difficult for people—and especially CEOs, not many of whom are known for their modest egos—to admit that they might be part of the problem. But they must do so if they want to establish a genuine sense of partnership between themselves and their managers.

• *Share the pain.* Middle managers feel exposed and vulnerable. When something goes wrong, they take the hit. And they can't help noticing that residents of the executive suite seem to emerge unscathed, even when they may be largely responsible for what has happened.

Some CEOs—but all too few—believe that they should share the hardship and sacrifice. Two of these are Ken Iverson and Herb Kelleher. Iverson, president of Nucor, a North Carolina steel company, took a 60 percent pay cut when his company's business suffered a downturn. And Kelleher, CEO of Southwest Airlines, voluntarily gave up 20 percent of his income—and reduced all officers' income by 10 percent.

• *Be candid with managerial candidates.* There's no more effective way to widen the trust gap than for a company to mislead promising managerial candidates about what it can offer them. To attract and retain good managers, a company must play straight with them.

While with Grow Group, Inc., Teresa McCaslin designed an approach to managerial candidates that was open and candid:

> We were basically honest with candidates, telling them that we were looking for entrepreneurial people and were very flat in terms of management levels. The good news, we said, is that they would have more access to higher levels of management for presentations and other contacts that could help their own development. But we didn't tell them they would definitely be going up six steps on a career ladder, because a year from now we might not even have that ladder, either because the positions weren't there or we had a different need to fill. We emphasized to both new and existing managers that there were different career moves they could make.
>
> This honesty helps in attracting good managers. They're not dumb—if you tell them they'll be here forever and go up the ladder, they'll know you're giving them a snow job. I think the honesty of saying you can't guarantee anything attracts the kinds of people you want: those who are interested in a challenge rather than a security blanket.

IS THE PACE TOO FAST?

Pressure. Twelve-hour days. Stress. Burnout. That's the way middle management jobs are described today. Of course, many people in management and the professions have always worked long hours. But now there's a qualitative difference. *Fortune* reports that a Harvard MBA asked his father, a retired lawyer, how he had managed to cope with *his* high-powered job. His father replied, "You mean you *don't* take a nap every day after lunch?"

Why are today's managerial jobs so stressful? Here are some answers:

- Today's managers work in a far more unstable, fluctuating environment than yesterday's did. There is more stress because managers constantly face new, ever-changing problems, while their predecessors dealt with basically the same problems every day.
- Today's managers no longer take explicit, clear-cut orders from above and execute them according to well-established procedures. Instead, they must define what tasks are critical and be innovative in performing them.
- In flattened organizations, managers must shoulder the burden of work that was done by other managers who are no longer around. This problem could be eased through sound restructuring. But a study by University of Michigan business professor Kim Cameron of 30 industrial companies shows that in most restructurings companies fail to rebalance the work load among survivors. Cameron told *Fortune:* "The general approach is to throw a hand grenade at a bunch of employees, and whoever survives has to do all the work there was before."
- Organizations are pushing their managers harder in a struggle to keep up with global competition.
- And then there's the stress of wondering whether you'll still have a job next week.

Middle-manager stress has its price, both for the managers and the organizations in which they work. According to the New York Business Group on Health, Inc., the annual cost to U.S. employers in absenteeism, reduced productivity and efficiency, morale problems, and alcohol and substance abuse is between $50 billion and $75 billion. Absenteeism alone is a major factor: Employees with stress-related disorders lose an average of 16 days a year from work, says a national Gallup survey.

It wasn't supposed to be like this. For years, futurists predicted that managerial jobs would be easier and require shorter hours because of new technology that would save time and effort. It hasn't worked out that way. True, new technology is producing information faster and faster. But that's part of the problem. Information has to be acted upon—and the faster it is produced, the faster something must be done with it. Computers spew out lengthy documents which can then be transmitted instantaneously by fax machine to any place in the world. No longer is there the luxury of days before getting a response. Instead, the response comes back without any wait, requiring more action immediately. This is one reason why today's middle managers work, on average, one day's worth of hours more every week than they did in 1980.

CAN WE LOWER THE HIGH ANXIETY?

Middle-manager stress cannot be eliminated—it comes with the territory. And stress can be healthy—up to a point. But when it is pervasive and extreme, it can be dangerously destructive. Julie A. Cohen, in *Management Review,* points out that overstress can result in sleep disturbances, loss of energy, difficulty in concentrating, loss of interest in work, frequent absenteeism, nervousness, irritability, and fear. Managers suffering such symptoms are not likely to be helping their organization much.

Despite this, not too many CEOs seem to be overly concerned about the stress in their middle-management ranks. They are constantly dealing with stressful situations themselves, so they see no reason why their managers should complain about it. What they may overlook is that middle managers, while facing stress as they do, are not as well positioned to cushion the effects. Perhaps if middle managers had chauffeured limousines to ride in, company jets to travel in, executive dining rooms to relax in, and a squad of underlings to do their bidding, they might not feel quite so overstressed. Even more important, if they had the sense of control of the CEO, the stress could be absorbed.

Top management ignores middle-manager stress at its own peril. Burned-out, alienated managers are not going to help the organization meet its global competition. The best of them will leave for what they hope are greener pastures. And those who stay will be a drag on the organization's ability to be innovative and productive—and to provide the customer service that should be the core of any company's strategy.

A few companies are beginning to deal with the stress problems of their employees. For example, A.T.&T. has "stress-down days" when employees come to work wearing casual clothes, including jeans and sweatshirts. And Apple Computer offers lessons in *aikido* massage on the premises, and an equestrian club to help overstressed employees unwind.

Admirable as these initiatives may be, they are "Band-Aid" solutions to a far deeper problem that requires more radical, innovative solutions.

STEPPING OFF THE FAST TRACK

Although there are many aspects of the Japanese business culture that are worth emulating, most middle managers would agree that *karoshi* is not one of them. That's understandable, since *karoshi* means "death from overwork." As the 80s came to a close, the subject began to stimulate great controversy in Japan. In 1989, according to the *Japan Times,* more than 1,300 families sought advice on filing claims against companies contending that the death of their relatives was caused by overwork. In response, the Japanese government agreed to begin a $2 million study to determine whether working in a Japanese office can cause *karoshi*.

In Japanese corporate culture, reports Steven Sabotta, an American living in Japan, "presence is productivity, loyalty to the organization is measured by time at one's desk, and employees are reluctant to be seen leaving the office. . . . The behavior resulting from these attitudes is the cause of *karoshi.*"

It would be extreme to say that the United States is facing an imminent *karoshi* epidemic. But as we head into the 1990s, there are danger signs on the horizon. Some middle managers are succumbing to the same fears as their Japanese counterparts. Listen to Robert Paulson, director of McKinsey & Co.'s Los Angeles office: "It's like two aging gunslingers squaring off to go at it. Both of them would be happy to go off and have an ice cream soda together, but neither one wants to be the first to blink."

What might be called "fear of leaving the office" is not groundless. A poll of 206 CEOs done for *Fortune* by Clark Martire & Bartolomeo revealed that 53 percent expected their middle managers to work between 50 and 59 hours a week—and 9 percent expected them to work 60 to 69 hours.

Perhaps these CEOs should consider whether raw hours spent at work are a valid measure of *productivity* at work. A middle manager's presence on the job does not necessarily mean that the manager is functioning effectively. To the contrary, longer work hours can result in lowered efficiency and productivity.

Morale is also a problem. Middle managers may be working longer hours—but many of them aren't happy about it. Data suggests that middle managers are having second thoughts about measuring up to the high-commitment profile that has been ordained for them by their leaders. Instead, they want to achieve a more equitable balance between their work lives and their personal lives. Such a balance is not possible when a manager leaves the house at 6 A.M., gets home at 8 P.M., and, after grabbing something to eat, sits down at a home computer.

A survey of 1,000 employees by the San Francisco-based recruiting firm Robert Half International is revealing. When asked to choose between a career path with flexible hours and more family time but slower career advancement and one with greater time demands but faster career progression, nearly 8 out of 10 opted for the slower, family-oriented path. Moreover, two out of three said they'd be willing to reduce their salaries to gain more family and personal time.

A company that addresses these needs will be better able to attract and retain valuable middle managers. What can it do?

First, recognize the needs—and that they apply to both men and women. Although much of the controversy over alternative career paths has revolved around women, the same issues apply to men. Perhaps the "mommy track" should be renamed the "mommy-daddy track." Even this label is too limiting, however. Career tracks should be applied to individuals, not to groups. Some want to be hard-chargers and commit their lives to their work. Some don't. And some may change their minds in midstream. Unless management recognizes these individual needs, it's going to have a lot of middle managers working (or not working) in the wrong jobs.

Most companies still find it difficult to acknowledge that it's not only their female employees who have family concerns. Old stereotypes hang on far beyond the time when the realities dictate that they should be discarded. As Betty Holcomb, senior editor of *Working Mother,* says: "Employees are still measured by the clock, as if Donna Reed stood watch in every home to care for the sick children, meet the plumber, and run the errands."

The fact is that Donna Reed isn't home anymore to do all those things—she's out earning a paycheck (and on the way home, making quick stops to pick up a microwavable meal at the supermarket and her child at the day-care center). Seventy percent of women with children between 6 and

17, and 50 percent of women with children less than 1 year old, are in the labor force. With the changing role of women in our society, the old image of the male breadwinner who has no family obligations except to bring home a salary check every week just doesn't fly.

Recent data make this clear. Du Pont, for example, conducted a study on work and family in 1985 and again in 1988. It found that in 1988, male employees were considerably more concerned about family-related problems—such as relocation and finding last-minute child care—than they were in 1985. Says Faith Wohl, director of Du Pont's Work Force Partnering Division: "We have found dramatic evidence that the men's attitudes toward work-family questions are very quickly coming to resemble women's." And *Working Mother's* Betty Holcomb reports that the Los Angeles Department of Water and Power recently found that its male employees had more problems with child care than did its female employees—to the tune of about $1 million a year in absenteeism costs.

Nor is it only a question of dealing with child-care emergencies. Male middle managers are becoming more concerned about being better parents. Many remember their own childhood, when daddy was the invisible man who left the house before they got up and didn't get home until after they were in bed. But as these managers are pushed harder and harder, they find themselves being forced into the same pattern.

Companies will discover that if they don't acknowledge and address these problems, their best middle managers will leave them for companies that do.

Among these companies is Honeywell. In its human resources guide entitled "Work and Family," used by its business units in establishing their employee policies and practices, the company has come up with a remarkable statement of what it believes it must do to attract and retain the talent it needs to attain its business objectives. Although every company must develop policies tailored to its own business, the Honeywell policies can serve as a useful springboard:

Work and Family

Changing demographics in our labor markets as well as within Honeywell, combined with changing employee expectations, have created the need to develop and implement appropriate means of accommodating employee issues and support a balance between job and business requirements and family responsibilities within the workplace environment.

Key trends, developments, and employee attitudes both within and external to the company are undisputable and include:

- Women and minority employees will form, by far, the largest segments of our work force in the near future.
- Two-income families, many with children, have become and will remain the norm.
- Labor shortages will occur in certain industry segments and job families as the "baby boom" generation ages, requiring the tapping of different labor markets, the retention of older workers, and so on.
- Longevity will increase the magnitude of employees' eldercare considerations.
- Employees have shown an increasing unwillingness to sacrifice family considerations to job or career tradeoffs.
- Employees have or will be faced with less counterproductive stress if they are supported in achieving a balance between work and family issues.

As an employer, our ability to develop and maintain an environment that allows employees to balance their work with their family and personal considerations is becoming crucial to the achievement of business objectives including:

- *Productivity improvement:* Accommodating employee needs with as much flexibility as possible will nearly always serve to address employee stress in balancing work and family issues and allow individuals to be more productive.
- *Attraction and retention of necessary talent:* A competitive advantage in recruitment and retention can be gained by providing practices and programs that recognize and

address the employees' family and personal considerations. Also, in view of potential labor shortages, well-conceived and executed practices, such as innovative work schedules, may allow business units to better tap certain labor "markets" (employees with school-age children, older workers, two-career families).

• *Work force diversity:* Increasingly diverse needs and expectations of our work force will require creative and flexible solutions to best accommodate and maximize the utilization and development of such a work force.

Honeywell's guide goes on to outline the minimally acceptable corporate standards on which its business units must base their detailed policies, practices, and procedures on dependent care, long-term leaves, vacation, short-term illness, personal leaves, alternative work arrangements, travel and overtime, information resources, and community involvement.

Honeywell is thus dealing openly with issues that were never even discussed in the days of the old unwritten contract between middle managers and their companies. Under the old contract, the manager had to fit the job. Honeywell, among other farsighted companies, realizes that now the job must be adapted to the manager. Michael Maccoby, president of The Maccoby Group, points out that just as products and services are being customized, companies will have to customize work arrangements, providing, for example, flexible schedules for new-generation managers.

IBM, Johnson & Johnson, NCNB, Du Pont, and Eastman Kodak are examples of other companies that have taken steps to accommodate employee needs. NCNB's "Select Time" program gives its middle managers (and other employees) the option of reducing their time and job commitments for dependent-care purposes—without harming their current and future advancement opportunities. IBM allows certain employees to take up to a three-year sabbatical from full-time employment, with part-time work during the second and third years.

Finding the Balance

IBM is one of the few forward-thinking companies that have begun to recognize the need to help managers find ways to balance the demands of career and family life. In 1988 the company offered innovative leave-of-absence and flex-time programs.

IBM's expanded personal leave-of-absence program allows employees to continue to receive company-paid benefits while on leave and to be assured of a job when they return. Those who need time for child care may choose to work part-time at IBM during the first year and must be available to work part-time during the second and third years, depending on the company's needs. Employees can do their part-time work at home, provided they spend at least four consecutive hours each week at their regular work site.

IBM's flex-time program allows employees to begin work up to an hour before or after the normal location start time and then put in a full day.

IBM news release, October 17, 1988.

Apple Computer's Deborah Biodolillo, vice president of human resources, says that her company's work culture is based on flexible structures that support a changing work force, market, and economy. In her words:

> We don't expect a lifetime commitment from our employees, but we have created an exciting, flexible environment that allows us to attract and retain the most talented individuals in the technology industry. We've done this by providing options—from job sharing to day care to sabbaticals. There are no "tracks" at Apple, only individual paths based on the choices our employees make in balancing career and personal needs. Some choose to emphasize their careers first; others, their families. But many choose both—and are successful in doing so.

Tailoring jobs to individual needs is not without its problems. One that many companies find troublesome is the issue of fairness. This was less of an issue when employers applied their personal policies across the board to all their employees. They could always say to an employee who wanted special accommodations: "We can't do that for you because then we'd have to do it for everyone."

So personnel decisions were much easier. Then management could go by the book—now it must decide on the basis of individual needs. And this is an uncomfortable role for any employer that up until now has had an inflexible, bureaucratic culture.

Middle managers can no longer be treated as if they all came out of the same mold. But managers with similar needs should be given similar work accommodations to the extent that it is practically possible, given the circumstances of their units. Honeywell, for example, tells its business units that they should "maximize flexibility in addressing individual needs and allowing for employee choice, rather than dictating narrow options." At the same time, Honeywell says, there must be a reasonable consistency in the application of policies and practices—and accommodations must be worked out according to both the needs of the individual and the needs of the business.

THE MANAGERIAL CONTRIBUTION

Top management can't do it all. There will be no partnership unless middle managers contribute to making it work. What can they do?

Richard Chagnon of Right Associates hits on one key point:

> In our advice to managers, we ask them to think in terms of their "locus of control." Are they sitting in the back seat, being driven somewhere (external locus of control), or are they behind the steering wheel, making their own decisions, checking the map, and taking charge of where they're going (internal locus of control)? We're saying that controlling their

own destiny is a lot healthier and more effective than sitting in the back seat and waiting for someone else to figure out what you have to do.

Chagnon zeros in on a fundamental change that must occur if middle managers and their companies are to develop a new partnership: Managers must become more autonomous. This may seen paradoxical, since any partnership involves a certain amount of interdependence. But in reality it makes perfect sense. Only when middle managers become more autonomous will they be *free* to enter into a new partnership that puts them on a more equal footing with their companies. They will not depend on their companies for their very existence, nor necessarily for the central core of their lives as they so often did in the past. Instead, they will depend on their companies for certain conditions and rewards while they are there—and if the company fails in its part of the bargain, they will be in a far better position to seek alternatives. But managers must keep *their* part of the bargain as long as they remain with the company. This is the nature of the new compact: fair, aboveboard, committed, energetic, and faithful on both sides—but no longer "until death (or retirement) do us part."

Ironically, the most effective way for managers to contribute to this new partnership is to put enlightened self-interest to work rather than to think in terms of sacrifice. In the past, many managers submerged their personal identities and their free wills to give their blind loyalty to the corporations that fed and sheltered them. This was not a true partnership, any more than the relationship between a trained bear and its master is. A true partnership can flourish only when both parties are gaining what they want from the relationship.

Managers who feel trapped and powerless are not inclined to form a new partnership with their employers. Their mind-set is that of a reluctant participant rather than a willing partner. A partnership can be formed only when *both* parties are dealing from strength as they work out a

win-win relationship. So the new contract must run something like this:

Company: "While you are here, we will do the best we can to
help you grow and achieve your goals if you help to
achieve ours, but we will also keep our options open
because the future is uncertain. Meanwhile, we will
share with you our best estimates of our future and
yours."

Manager: "While I am here, I will give you my best efforts if you
consider my needs and goals along with yours, but I
will also keep my options open, because I know there
are no guarantees no matter how well I perform."

Let's repeat a point made in the preceding chapter: The
impetus for change must come from corporate leadership.
The chief executive must take the initiative in closing the
trust gap and forging this new partnership with the company's middle managers. Lacking a corporate environment
that fosters credibility and trust, middle managers will have
no incentive to commit themselves to a partnership or to
their company.

But once top management credibly demonstrates that it
is ready to provide such an environment, managers can
make their own contribution to the new partnership. However, this may require some basic attitudinal changes and
some new initiatives.

Old Expectations versus New Realities

Although there are many things a company can do to foster
a new partnership with its managers, there are certain
things it *cannot* do, simply because they are beyond its control. Only when managers recognize and accept these realities will there be any basis for a partnership. Here are some
caveats for the manager:

Don't look to your company for financial security. As
John L. Sprague, former president of Sprague Electric Company, puts it:

Part of the new contract is that middle managers must accept the realities of business today. Security can no longer come from a company. With the whole mergers and acquisitions game today, a company can be doing swimmingly well and then someone comes in and takes it over and wipes out a whole layer.

So security must come from the inside out. As an employer, I can help you improve your personal assets so you'll feel better about yourself. You won't worry so much about what the company does because you know that with these assets you're a desirable person in a lot of places. So you'll feel good about the company because it is providing you with an opportunity to become better qualified for what you think you want to do. Managers should look less for guarantees and more for self-development opportunities. Their loyalty isn't to the company; it is to their career and their acquisition of knowledge.

The truth is that security has always come from within. The best managers, even in the past, acted on this belief, and their self-confidence made them more independent in their thinking, and hence better contributors. But false organizational security was sought by many, if not most, managers. As Sprague says, since organizational security is now a thing of the past, today's managers must do what they can to provide their own security. This was not a worry under the old unwritten contract—middle managers knew (or thought) they could count on their regular paychecks until they retired and on their pensions for their remaining years. Now they know they can be out of a job tomorrow. Depending entirely on one's bimonthly paycheck is not only risky, but increases dependency on the corporation and can block one's thinking about career moves that could provide more work satisfaction, and sometimes a higher level of achievement.

Some managers are responding to the new uncertainty by building their own financial cushions. This can be done by building up savings, making profitable investments, or even by developing a second income.

Make the most of lateral mobility. Moving sideways may not seem as attractive as moving upward—and to some managers it will never be a satisfactory alternative. But for many middle managers, lateral movement is a reality that must be accepted, because flatter companies no longer have all those nice, high-sounding positions to which their managers can be promoted. Yet moving laterally can also be an opportunity, because it often provides managers with work choices that fit in with their personal goals and needs.

Being promoted has never guaranteed that one was moving to a better job. True, it means climbing higher on the organization chart and enjoying a bigger paycheck. But other aspects of the new job can often be less satisfactory. It might require much longer hours, snatching away time for family and other interests. There might be more traveling, which to many managers is probably the least satisfying aspect of their jobs. It might require relocation, something else that managers are increasingly resisting.

Moreover, corporate America's historic obsession with promotions has led in many cases to lowered productivity. A top-producing salesperson with great customer rapport who loved selling would be promoted to become a mediocre sales manager. Or a great manufacturing engineer would be "elevated" to the corporate quality-control staff, where he or she would not perform as well.

So there are some desirable trade-offs in giving up the traditional career ladder. Among them are:

- *The opportunity to learn a new job.* The more skills a manager can attain, the more career options that manager has—not a minor consideration in this era of job insecurity.
- *Less pressure on the job.* Some managers thrive in a pressure-cooker environment, but others prefer a less tortured work life. A lateral job move may be the answer for them—as well as for the company, which should constantly be seeking the best manager/job fit.

- *A more dynamic job working with stimulating people:* This is a possibility for the manager who does enjoy a fast-moving environment. The opportunity to deal with challenging situations can be worth more to that manager than the perks of promotion, especially in the long run.

Take individual responsibility for life and career planning. Companies are no longer going to design and implement well-defined career paths for their middle managers (if they ever really did!). Many, however, are willing to help managers work out their own do-it-yourself plans by providing job options and growth opportunities.

This shift of the career-planning burden to the shoulders of managers has a very positive side: It provides them with the opportunity to aim for what they *want* to do rather than what they are *required* to do to fit in with a career path that has been ordained for them by a human resources department or task force.

In the past, many managers simply fell into their jobs, often based on the advice and counsel of others. With the cradle-to-grave tradition of the old unwritten employment contract, they became trapped in these jobs even though the job provided no satisfaction beyond pay and security.

Therefore, one important clause in the new employment contract is that companies will no longer map out life-long careers for their middle managers. Many employers, including Eastman Kodak, have already made that shift. According to Cindy M. Cahill, retraining manager of the company's Kodak Park Division:

> Employees are expected to assume greater responsibilities for their own career development and quality of worklife. These responsibilities include:
> - Self-assessment of skills, interests, and values.
> - Reality checking—that is, finding out what is possible.
> - Establishing goals and taking action through development planning.

The manager's superior will not control this process, but
will play the role of coach: someone who shares information,
highlights options, provides feedback, and provides access to
resources and people.

These responsibilities for self-development involve a shift
in culture at Kodak. In the past, our company lived by a more
paternalistic philosophy of "Do a good job and trust us—we'll
take care of you." Today, we recognize that we don't know
enough to manage people's careers. We can, however, provide
the resources, information, and coaching necessary to support employees in managing their own careers.

This puts the ball squarely in the manager's court. How
managers respond to this challenge is an important key to
achieving a successful new contract with their companies.
Managers who take charge of their own career development
will not only be enhancing their growth and job satisfaction,
but also they will be more valuable to their employers. They
will, moreover, be less susceptible to job stress, a condition
that develops primarily from a feeling of little or no control
over one's environment.

What can managers do to begin taking control of their
own destiny? They might start by asking some basic questions about themselves:

1. *What are my strengths?* Am I using them on my
   present job? (A very good reason for making a lateral
   move is to be able to use strengths that are not usable in your current job.)
2. *What do I really enjoy doing?* Coaching, organizing,
   number crunching, problem solving, traveling, working alone, working with a team? Where and how
   have I succeeded in the past?
3. *What kind of an organization do I want to work
   in?* Small, entrepreneurial, fast-growing? Big, well-
   established, a market leader?
4. *How much responsibility do I want?* The more the
   better? Responsibility for my own work only? Flexibility to move up as I grow?

5. *What kinds of people do I like to work with?* Looking back, what people have I most enjoyed working with? How about least enjoyed?

6. *To what extent am I willing to give up my outside life for my job?* Are 60-hour work weeks okay, even though my social or family life will suffer? Or am I unwilling to sacrifice that outside time? What balance do I need?

7. *How much stress am I willing to take?* Too much stress is bad for anybody, but some people can take it better than others. Do I seek control, or am I amenable to being controlled?

8. *What is my personal definition of success?* Money? Power? Office perks? Challenging work? Self-actualization? A job I can look forward to getting up for in the morning? What trade-offs seem right for me?

9. *Are my behavioral characteristics compatible with the job requirements?* Can I be myself or must I fit into some externally imposed, cookie-cutter mold?

10. *How deeply felt are my ethical beliefs?* And how should they affect my choice of organization or job?

Dealing with Stress

It's a fact that middle managers must face: Their jobs are more stressful than in the past. Employers should be mindful of stress and find effective ways to alleviate its effects whenever they become acute. Doing so is in their self-interest because the anxiety caused by stress can cause managers to show less spontaneity and more rigidity, rely on safer responses, have reduced ability to improvise, and expend more effort to maintain adequate behavior.

Managers, for their part, must also take responsibility for dealing with stress. Only they know their own stress threshold. Often, the problem is not the stress itself—which can stimulate performance in moderate doses—but overreaction to it, emotionally and sometimes even physiologically.

To avoid these harmful effects of stress, writer Donald P. Huddle suggests these stress busters:

- *Try to get away from the job situation during the day, even if only briefly.* Don't pore over reports on your coffee break—do something unrelated to your job.
- *Take vacations—even short ones.* And occasionally, at least once a year, take a real one- or two-week break. For most managers, especially older ones, long weekends just won't do it.
- *Verbalize the problems that are causing stress and anxiety.* Talk to a colleague (whom you can trust to be discreet) or to a friend. Bottled-up anxiety is the worst kind—talking it out can give you a better perspective on the problem.
- *Exercise regularly.* Stress experts say that exercise conditions the body's stress-adaptation mechanisms. But make sure the exercise is regular, rather than frenzied activity every weekend. How about taking up exercise on your lunch hour?
- *Eat balanced meals as regularly as you can.* Erratic eating habits can aggravate the effects of stress.
- *Get periodic medical checkups.* They occasionally reveal problems of which you might be unaware that may be contributing to symptoms of overreaction to stress.
  BUT MOST IMPORTANT:
- Try to negotiate—as an *integral* part of your job—an adequate level of autonomy. Failing this, at least obtain a clear definition of how much control you will have over your work content, your deadlines, and your choice of employees in the unit you manage. Plan and negotiate this at the front end—once you are already in a low-control, high-stress job, it's difficult to bargain your way out of it. Remember: It is not hard work or long hours that create stress, but lack of control.

CHAPTER 10

FUTURE IMPERATIVE: THE NEW PARTNERSHIP

Businesses will undergo more, and more radical, restructuring in the 1990s than at any time since the modern corporate organization first evolved in the 1920s. . . . By now a great many—maybe most—large American companies have cut management levels by one third or more. But the restructuring of corporations—middle-sized ones as well as large ones, and, eventually, even smaller ones—has barely begun.
—Peter Drucker

Predicting the future is a risky business—about the only safe thing you can say is that it's ahead of us. But Peter Drucker's prediction (although he calls it a conclusion based on what is already happening) of continued and accelerated corporate restructuring seems a sound bet.

Clearly, the winning organization of tomorrow will be flatter than today's. As Drucker has been telling us for years, one force driving this change is the growing dominiance of knowledge workers, individuals who are able to exert their influence far beyond their assigned places on the organization chart. Another powerful flattening force is global competition, which makes organizational streamlining an imperative.

But while flatness is a necessary condition for future success, it is far from sufficient. Fleetness will be just as essential—nimbleness, speed of response, flexibility, and a willingness to experiment with new ways of doing everything.

One of the most important of these new ways is globalization. Already, some large U.S. multinationals garner almost one third of their revenues (and a higher portion of profits) from products manufactured overseas. The most successful companies seek out technological advances wherever they occur and have learned to use information strategically throughout their global operations.

Existing information technologies—electronic mail, facsimile transmission, on-line services, and satellite communications, for instance—serve to leverage the power of knowledge workers and can help to make U.S. organizations both efficiently flat and fleet of foot. Future blends of these and newer technologies—such as high-definition television, pocket computers, voice-operated computers, personal faxes, fiber-optic networks, and language-translation software—are sure to provide a quantum leap in information-handling capability. It is conceivable that some day we may be able virtually to ignore time-zone and foreign-language barriers—and national boundaries.

The economic and geopolitical world, too, is changing at a rapid pace. And we need not wait for Europe 1992 or China 1997 to note the effects of these shifts. In the automobile industry alone, some two dozen manufacturers are already engaged in almost 300 global alliances or joint ventures. According to former Chrysler Corporation Vice Chairman Gerald Greenwald, "No car company will be successful . . . that doesn't learn to develop strategic international alliances."

His observation is just as true of other industries. *Fortune* reports that American corporations have formed over 2,000 alliances with European companies alone. Corning, for example, now realizes more than half its earnings from joint

ventures, two thirds of which are with foreign partners. Today, even competitors forge alliances: Airbus Industrie with
Lockheed, Chrysler with Mitsubishi, Johnson & Johnson
with Merck, and Merck with DuPont.

The corporation of tomorrow must be highly diverse in
form and action. In fact, it could aptly be called the protean
corporation. In Greek mythology, the god Proteus was able to
change himself instantly into any form he wished—into fire
or water, for example. Endowed with vast stores of information and knowledge, he also had the gift of seeing the future.

As new markets emerge and more countries become major players in the global market, U.S. companies will need
such a vast scope of knowledge. But to use this knowledge
effectively, their tired old stonelike structures will not do.
They must dismantle their corporate pyramids and replace
them with information-rich networks of amorphous, ever-
changing form if they are to compete successfully in the
years to come. And they must do this in a consumer market
that will be much tougher and more complex—they must
satisfy consumers who demand quality products and better
service, and who refuse to be lumped together into a homog-
enous mass market.

The message is, then, that the 90s will be even more
challenging to U.S. business than the late, unlamented 80s.
As GE's Jack Welch has said, this will be a "white-knuckle
decade for global business." For any U.S. corporation to succeed will take even more than restructuring. It will also
take a force of high-performing managerial employees who
can produce the results needed to accomplish organizational
goals and strategies. A new partnership between managers
and their employers is desperately needed. The question is:
Will U.S. business leaders commit themselves to making
the major changes required to develop such a partnership?
Or, despite all their restructuring, will they embark on
short-lived fads and gimmicks rather than fundamental
change?

The answer, of course, is that we don't know. At this juncture, it is too early to lean strongly toward pessimism or optimism. Most corporations are just beginning to grapple with the realities that the futurists warned us we should have been addressing for the past 25 years. U.S. business is in the midst of shifting currents and conflicting forces. Its direction is uncertain, some would say chaotic. The very governance of companies is in a state of turbulence, and this governance can determine whether corporate management will provide the high quality of leadership that is demanded.

A key question that companies will tackle in the years ahead is: "Will we have less and less need for middle managers?" (Since the dawn of the information age, pundits have predicted that middle managers will be replaced by computers.) Our answer is no. True, U.S. companies became so fat that they had to waddle laboriously just to stay in place while their foreign competitors were running circles around them. There was no escaping the truth: Because of their prescribed bureaucratic roles, middle managers often slowed things down rather than speeding them up. Under the pressure of accelerating technology and aggressive competition, employers found it imperative to eliminate unneeded layers of management that were crippling the ability to move swiftly in response to market changes.

But during the 1980s, hundreds of thousands of middle management jobs were eliminated for reasons that were less praiseworthy. The profusion of mergers, acquisitions, takeovers, and leveraged buyouts loaded companies so heavily with debt that they had to cut costs drastically to produce the cash flow needed just to service the debt. Management jobs were eliminated not in the name of efficiency but simply to save money. Number-crunching was substituted for strategic thinking and understanding of the business. Whenever decisions are made strictly on the basis of bottom-line arithmetic, human beings get crunched along with the numbers.

As we entered the 1990s, the decimation was continuing. In April 1990 *The Wall Street Journal* reported that "another surge of layoffs has begun, reflecting the effects of the junk bond market's slide and retailers' troubles, as well as further corporate retrenchments." In the first quarter of 1990, staff reductions totaled more than 110,000 people (equal to the figure for *all* of 1989!)—and these cutbacks hit all sectors of the economy.

Moreover, many companies were no longer offering early-retirement incentives to cut their staffs because they didn't want to lose their best people. Instead they were terminating people outright, and some were offering incentive packages aimed at retaining their key talent.

At the same time, increasing concern was voiced from some quarters that cutting management staff to the bone could be self-defeating. Executive headhunter Robert Brudno, for one, believed that such extensive dismissals would leave companies "not only lean and mean, but hobbled." *Business Week* wondered if U.S. business had gone too far: "Have they eliminated so many jobs that their operations are undermanaged? Will the new pressures on today's middle managers drive the most promising future leaders away from big companies? In their zeal to cut costs, have corporations overlooked the long-term benefits of nurturing an innovative, energetic corps of managers?"

WHAT FATE FOR MIDDLE MANAGERS?

Many observers say this is the end of an era for middle management. They're right. Nothing will ever be the same for middle managers again. But this could also be a whole new beginning—one that in many ways can make middle managers a more important force than before.

Whether this happens largely depends on the mind-set of America's corporate leaders as we traverse the 1990s. During the 80s decade, the corporate credo seemed to be: "The fewer middle managers the better." During the 90s, it might well be: "What is the new role of middle managers in our restructured organizations—and how can we maximize their value to the company?"

Looked at this way, the focus changes from elimination to optimization. The answer is not to dump middle managers overboard but to free them from bureaucratic restraints and build up their capacity to deal with tomorrow's business challenges.

Unfortunately, because so many top executives view their middle managers as liabilities rather than assets, there is a self-fulfilling prophecy at work in their companies. Whenever senior management believes that middle managers only serve to clog up the corporate arteries, that's exactly what they will probably do. But "corposclerosis" cannot be cured by magic pills. Only when management acts on the premise that its middle managers can be a powerful force in implementing company strategies will the results be different. There has been much talk about utilizing the potential of nonmanagerial employees to solve problems and generate ideas. Strangely, however, the companies that espouse this kind of employee involvement often don't apply the same approach to their middle managers. Through letters from the chairman or carefully crafted, video-delivered appeals, the work force is urged to follow the company's vision, while the left-out middle manager sees the appeals as hypocritical fluff or headquarters window dressing.

GE's Jack Welch put it well when he said, "Leaders have to find a better fit between their organization's needs and their people's capabilities. . . . Middle managers can be the stronghold of the organization. But their jobs have to be redefined."

For example, Walter Kiechel III suggests in *Fortune* that "the learning organization" model can offer a clearer and more important role "to the group most beaten up by restructuring—middle managers." Basically, the learning organization is one that constantly strives to do things better in an uncertain environment, rather than "minimizing risk, staying on plan, and making your numbers." According to Kiechel, the learning organization offers middle managers the major role in keeping the learning flowing throughout the company and integrating it for practical applications.

The concept of the learning organization is not new. In 1968 Robert M. Hutchins proposed "the learning society," in which all men and women, of whatever age, would have the opportunity to continue their education to achieve their full potential.

Regrettably, American society today falls far short of Hutchins's vision. Our kindergarten-through-12th-grade school systems have been studied, blue-chip commissioned, and task-forced for more than a decade. At educational summit meetings, state governors and members of the Federal Administration have pontificated and pointed fingers. Hundreds of corporations have initiated efforts to aid public education.

Yet America's number of functional illiterates, many of them in the workplace, is an ongoing national shame and disgrace. Corporations exist within this sad milieu. High-tech companies bemoan the shortage of hundreds of thousands of Ph.D.s trained in science and engineering, and even low-tech companies come up short in recruiting workers proficient in reading, writing, and simple arithmetic.

So we face the monumental challenge of developing a learning organization in an inadequately schooled society that seems to place other values higher on its priority list than education. Even so, there are corporations that serve as models of learning organizations: General Electric, IBM, and Merck, to name just three examples. But which companies, if any, are concentrating on middle managers as the catalysts for learning, teaching, and coaching?

Examples of such companies are difficult to find, and among those making the effort it is too early to gauge the results. In many companies there is a vast gap between the image and what is really going on. A two-year probe by the Massachusetts Institute of Technology found that U.S. business was afflicted by short time horizons and neglect of human resources. Among middle managers who recognize the need for changes, there is a foreboding that their present top management is either unable or unwilling to carry out those changes.

If these managers are right, U.S. business is in deep trouble. But this pessimism is offset by forces that are driving at least some companies to invest more heavily in their managerial and other human resources, rather than looking at them as costs that must be reduced.

One of these forces is the accelerating labor shortage. By 1990 companies were already beginning to feel the impact of this shortage on their ability to fill open positions. In a nationwide survey of employers by the American Society for Personnel Administration in the late 1980s, almost half of 700 respondents described difficulties in recruiting qualified managers. Early in 1990, *The Wall Street Journal* reported that a number of companies faced a shortage of managers with leadership and technical abilities. No wonder: Hundred of thousands had been "outplaced" just when they were needed.

It is premature, then, to conclude that middle managers will become an extinct species during the 1990s. They will still be important players in the corporate game—but this will be a new game with an entirely different set of rules. The manager of the future will bear little resemblance to the "corpocratic" model of the past:

Past: Strict adherence to boss-subordinate relationships.
Future: Hierarchical relationships subordinated to functional and peer relationships (in fact, the terms *boss* and *subordinate* may—and should—disappear from corporate vocabularies.

Past: Getting things done by giving orders.

Future: Getting things done by negotiating.

Past: Carrying messages up and down.

Future: Solving problems and making decisions.

Past: Performing a prescribed set of tasks according to a job description.

Future: Creating the job by developing entrepreneurial projects.

Past: Narrow functional focus.

Future: Broad cross-functional collaboration.

Past: Going through channels, one by one by one.

Future: Emphasizing speed and flexibility.

Past: Controlling subordinates.

Future: Coaching one's people.

VISION FOR THE FUTURE: A NEW PARTNERSHIP

Let us look ahead to the year 2000. Where will the relationship between middle managers and their employers be by then? Still in the depths of disillusionment, distrust, and disharmony? Will middle managers feel they are being used and abused, lied to and ignored, dumped on, then dumped?

We prefer another vision. Not Utopia, certainly, but a dramatic improvement in the relationship that disintegrated so badly during the 1980s. Improvement could happen—but only in the company that commits itself to doing the things that will close the trust gap, such as:

- Being honest with middle managers (and everyone else), thus earning credibility.
- Communicating with middle managers broadly and honestly.
- Creating a desirable work environment.
- Listening to middle managers and seeking their candid input.

- Giving middle managers recognition for their accomplishments.
- Doing everything possible to provide managers with challenging work.
- Helping middle managers to broaden their skills portfolios.
- Treating middle managers who must be terminated fairly and with respect.
- Communicating sound and understandable corporate objectives and explaining how middle managers can help to accomplish them.
- Bringing middle managers into the strategic planning process—which can help *top management* avoid major mistakes.
- Building constructive dissent into the decision-making process.
- Giving middle managers more control over their own activities.
- Providing middle managers with a piece of the action financially.
- Developing a corporate culture that encourages and enables employees to succeed.
- Striking a fair balance between individual and organizational goals.
- Recognizing that middle managers in the 90s are less willing than their managerial forebears to sacrifice other important aspects of their lives to their jobs.
- Acting upon the premise that a new partnership must be based on *shared information—up and down*.
- Sharing the sacrifice when the business hits hard times.
- Encouraging creativity and risk taking, without fear of punishment for failing.
- Including older managers in development efforts as well as younger ones.
- *Living* the ethical standards that it preaches.
- Developing customized work arrangements based on individual needs and goals.

- Compensating managers in ways that truly relate pay to performance—and consulting with them as the pay package is being designed.
- Providing learning opportunities, through formal internal and external training and on-the-job coaching.
- Making career development a genuinely two-way process—giving managers a greater say in their own development planning and implementation.

DOES IT REALLY MATTER?

So what if we don't make these changes? Who cares about middle managers, anyway? Some business pundits maintain that American companies, after dumping a third of their middle managers, are turning themselves around successfully by hard work, sharply lowered costs, and improved product quality—without all those middle managers who were cluttering up the landscape.

These pundits point to the new and highly hailed "bossless" work team as signing the death warrant for middle managers. In early 1990, a *Fortune* article asked this question: "Who needs a boss?" Not employees who work in self-managed teams, was the answer. Such teams "arrange schedules, buy equipment, fuss over quality—and dramatically boost the productivity of their companies." What makes "superteams" so controversial, the article went on, is "that they ultimately force managers to do what they had only imagined in their most Boschian nightmares: give up control."

It is true that, for certain types of complex jobs, self-managed teams without supervisors can go a long way toward improving morale, along with results. These superteams bring together individuals with different jobs or different functions, hence cutting through the organizational barriers between marketing, engineering design, manufacturing, and finance. But superteams are not totally unsupervised. For example, here's the way they work at Texas Instruments:

> On top is a steering team consisting of the plant manager and his heads of manufacturing, finance, engineering, and human resources. They set strategy and approve large projects. Beneath the steering team, TI has three other teams: corrective-action teams, quality-improvement teams, and effectiveness teams. The first two are cross-functional and consist mainly of middle managers and professionals like engineers and accountants. Corrective-action teams form to tackle short-lived problems and then disband. They're great for those times when, as the technophantasmic novelist Thomas Pynchon writes, there's fecoventilatory collision: the s – – – hits the fan.

Note, however, the composition of these bossless teams: mostly middle managers and knowledge workers. The latter often manage projects through persuasion and skill, though they may not supervise people hierarchically. So if the future success of American corporations depends partly upon our ability to create autonomous work teams—as we believe it does—middle managers are still vital contributors.

Then there's the "vision thing," an overworked buzzword of the 80s. (A book acquisition editor for AMACOM, the publishing arm of the American Management Association, was recently overheard to say, "If I see one more manuscript about vision, I think I'll scream!") All the hype about corporate vision has obscured the fact that middle managers don't feel they are part of that vision—they've been left out, and they act accordingly.

Corporate vision is as important today as it was in the days of the visionaries who founded some of America's greatest business enterprises, such as E.I. du Pont de Nemours, Eastman Kodak, Ford Motor Company, General Electric, IBM, and Sears. But someone must implement and execute the vision. Without a committed group of middle managers willing and able to take responsibility for bringing the vision to life, the vision will not become a reality.

BUT MEANWHILE, WHERE ARE
WE HEADING?

What is happening in the American economy as the millenium year of 2000 approaches makes it clear that a sharp change in direction is needed from our corporate leaders if there is to be any chance of restoring trust between middle managers and employers.

The last decade of the 20th century began at a fast clip. Domestic mergers and acquisitions continued, and new records were set across many industries from food and tobacco (RJR Nabisco) to entertainment (Time Warner). Debt was stalking the corporate landscape like a grim specter. Some leveraged buyouts were in deep trouble and survived only through leveraged bustups. Others failed. Bankruptcy law and the workout industry presented the latest growth opportunities.

The outplacement industry also continued its sharp growth. At the American Management Association's 1990 Human Resources Conference and Exposition in San Francisco, two of the most popular booths were those of Drake Beam Morin and Right Associates, the two largest outplacement firms in the United States. Executives of both companies expressed great satisfaction in the number of human resources professionals they met and marketed services to during the Expo. Indeed, there was discussion about expanding the outplacement organizations' booths for the 1991 Exposition. Both organizations were also launching programs to deal with the problems of organizational survivors and to help renew the cultures of organizations that had significantly downsized.

The "rolling recession" kept on rolling along, rolling over the media and advertising businesses, Wall Street investment firms, the computer industry, and others (as it had earlier rolled over oil and real estate). It rolled across the Northeast (as it had earlier over the Southwest)—and many held their breath, fearing that just ahead was the old-fashioned kind of recession. Inflation began to reappear, forcing companies to think even more seriously about cost cutting—including more downsizing. The threat of "stagflation" raised its ugly head.

On Wall Street, Michael Milken confessed to cheating, mail fraud, and other felonies—and plea-bargained his way to a $600 million fine. Meanwhile, however, many of his former fellow Drexel Burnham Lambert employees were walking the streets. Sporting the Drexel logo—especially on a résumé—was described as like being branded with a scarlet letter. The sins of their employers had been visited upon these outplaced employees.

And what was happening to the trust gap? Was the breach finally being closed? Hardly. Each springtime brings reports of executive pay for the preceding year. In the spring of 1990, *Business Week* reported the 1989 records, headed by Craig O. McCaw, the 40-year-old chief executive of McCaw Cellular, whose total pay exceeded $53.9 milion. Apparently trailing far behind was Steven J. Ross, co-chairman of Time Warner, who had made only $34.2 million. But not to worry—on January 10, 1990, Ross collected $75 million in cash, and as *Business Week* added, "there's plenty more where that came from. Some $92.6 million in cash remains piled up in a trust fund in Ross's name for payment to him in the years ahead."

Chrysler Corporation rejuvenator and supersalesman Lee Iacocca garnered more than $25 million in 1989 and received the dubious honor of being rated, for the third successive year, as the CEO who had provided shareholders the least for his pay.

Some executives wanted to be rewarded not only for the job they were doing (or not doing) but also for their accomplishments over their whole careers. Roger B. Smith, retiring chairman of General Motors, had taken over GM's helm in 1981, when that company's share of the U.S. car market was about 46 percent. By 1989 GM's share had wilted to 35 percent, most of the gap being filled by foreign cars. But in May 1990, General Motors' board sought to increase Smith's annual retirement pension from $700,000 to about $1.25 million, evidently as a reward for the job he had done. One reporter calculated this as about $600 per hour for each 40-hour week Smith *won't* work. (Or, another way of looking at it, $50,000 a year for each point of market share lost by GM during Smith's tenure.)

Since not only Smith had provided leadership to his corporation, his board also sought to increase the pensions of another 3,500 GM executives. This new plan will apply a pension formula to the bonuses of these top executives, including Smith, rather than only to their salaries.

The bonuses themselves had already created controversy during the 1980s and had created tension with the United Auto Workers, especially since GM had temporarily replaced annual salary increases for their workers with annual bonuses, thereby saving the corporation money and creating an even larger gap between the compensation of its workers and its senior executives.

As the compensation gap between workers and executives was extended beyond their worklives, the trust gap widened even further. Cradle-to-grave security seemed on the way to being succeeded by a cradle-to-grave trust gap. And there was little that employees or even shareholders could do about it. Indeed, GM's proxy statement specified that the pension proposal did not require approval by shareholders but could be passed by directors. (And at about the same time as the pension announcement, GM reported a 54 percent drop in quarterly income.)

During the 1980s, not all CEOs' compensation increased each year. There was much talk about pay for performance. So when IBM's 1989 profits plunged by 35 percent, CEO

John Akers' compensation decreased by 3 percent, bringing his annual compensation level from just above $2 million to just below $2 million—evidently the executive suite's idea of "sharing the pain." Even at IBM there was a yawning gap between its top executives' pensions and those of its managers.

IBM's current situation is in sharp contrast to the philosophy that had been the foundation of IBM's first pension plan. In 1945, just 12 days after the end of World War II, Thomas J. Watson, Sr., addressed a group of employees at IBM's Endicott, New York, plant. During the war, this plant had manufactured weapons and other war materials. In a speech designed to motivate IBM employees to reconvert efficiently to commercial products, Watson thanked them for their magnificent efforts during the war and announced the company's first pension plan, to be principally funded by the earnings that Watson himself had received during the war from IBM's weapons production.

Remarkably, every IBM employee was to receive the same pension—regardless of earnings level. Watson reasoned that managers who earned far more money during their careers didn't need higher pensions because they had ostensibly put away a nest egg for retirement. (They don't do it that way at IBM anymore.)

GETTING RID OF PRECIOUS CARGO

A striking analogy with today's downsizing era can be found in the 1990 novel *The Horse Latitudes*. Author Robert Ferrigno explains the title this way:

> The horse latitudes was an area in the Atlantic Ocean where the trade winds died, becalming sailing ships on their journey to the New World. The most severe and profound doldrums could be escaped only by abandoning their most precious cargo—horses. Once these frightened animals were pushed over the side, the sails began to fill. The horses swam after the ships for miles before they drowned. The screams of those horses haunted the sailors the rest of the voyage.

In the 1980s, too many captains of America's corporate ships off-loaded their own precious cargo: their people. Possibly they neglected to remember that the crew, unlike the horses, helps to run the ship.

Direction—and vision—from the bridge is essential, but not enough. Someone must work in the engine room; someone must staff the ship; someone must serve the passengers. Or there won't be any passengers. Or any voyage.

A ship's crew is hierarchically structured, but a great ship enjoys crew members who go beyond their prescribed jobs. The same is true of the people in any great corporation. To move a corporation forward in today's roily waters requires the full commitment of men and women in middle management roles.

To obtain that commitment, senior executives must act on three simple premises:

- Middle managers are motivated in the same way that top managers are motivated: through challenge, accomplishment, recognition, and reward.
- Middle managers want to be treated as intelligent, worthy human beings.
- Middle managers recognize fairness—and unfairness, as do all employees.

We know these things in our minds and in our guts. But too often we fail to act upon what we know. The trust gap, that great abyss that sets employees against employer, was created by American management's failure to act upon these beliefs and convictions—and, instead, their indulgence in quick fixes and by-the-numbers management.

As a result, we have broken a sacred covenant between employers and their managers, an agreement that tacitly but strongly existed for three decades, a 30-year period of remarkable growth in America's standard of living that made us the envy of the world. To go beyond that broken covenant, to close that trust gap, corporate leadership must take deliberate actions and *sustain* them.

Creating a new partnership will be neither easy nor quick. This book's intent has been to outline the elements that must go into forging this new partnership. Earlier in this chapter, we outlined our vision of a dramatically improved relationship and what must be done to close the trust chasm—two dozen guidelines that provide a road map of the new partnership.

While these guidelines are important, what is most important is the degree of commitment by CEOs to a belief in the worth of the individual—and a willingness to trust middle managers and other employees. Unless corporate leaders trust them, they will never trust their leaders—it will always be them versus us.

SIGNING THE NEW CONTRACT

The new contract between employers and their middle managers will not be based on legalities but on trust and respect. It will be an unwritten contract, so it can only be signed—and faithfully carried out—through the behavior of both parties. For its part, the company must have a clearly articulated human resources philosophy that is *fully supported by practices, decisions, and actions.* For their part, managers must exercise unprecedented flexibility, manage their own expectations, and be prepared for any eventuality without succumbing to fear of sudden change. Both must accept together the challenge of becoming partners in the effort to improve their organization's ability to adapt and compete.

ENDNOTES

CHAPTER 1

Page

4   They are the ones of our middle class: Whyte, William Jr. *The Organization Man*. Simon & Schuster, 1956, p. 3.

5   When (college seniors) explained: Whyte. *The Organization Man*, p. 71.

5   As *Training* editor Jack Gordon put it: Gordon, Jack. "Who Killed Corporate Loyalty." *Training*, March 1990, p. 25.

6   Surveys by Right Associates: "Middle Managers Hurt Most by Job Squeeze—Survey," *Human Resource Reporter*, February 24, 1989.

6   *The Wall Street Journal* estimated: Kanter, Rosabeth Moss. "The Contingent Job and the Post-Entrepreneurial Career." *Management Review*, April 1989, p. 22.

7   In the third quarter of 1989: Bennett, Amanda. "Business Takes Out Its Trimming Shears." *The Wall Street Journal*, October 5, 1989, page A2.

7   In late 1989: White, Joseph B. "GM Plans to Cut Its White-Collar Work Force 25%." *The Wall Street Journal*, November 22, 1989, page A3.

7   At the end of the year: Schellhardt, Timothy D., and Amanda Bennett. "White-Collar Layoffs Open 1990, and May Close It, Too." *The Wall Street Journal*, January 15, 1989, p. B1.

10   The dominant mood: Castro, Janice. "Where Did the Gung-Ho Go?" *Time*, September 11, 1989, p. 53.

10   In a 1989 Yankelovich Clancy Shulman survey: Castro. "Where Did the Gung-Ho Go?" p. 54.

12   Two Opinion Research surveys: Farnham, Alan. "The Trust Gap." *Fortune*, December 4, 1989, p. 57.

13   Idea entrepreneurs will receive: Kanter, Rosabeth Moss. "The Reshaping of Middle Management." *Management Review*, January 1986, p. 19.

16   As David Halberstam points out: Halberstam, David. "The End of the Feast." *Best of Business Quarterly*, Winter 1989–1990, p. 34.

Page

16 As Robert Tomasko pointed out: Tomasko, Robert M. *Downsizing.* New York: AMACOM, 1987.

17 In 1969 American manufacturers: Schellhardt, Timothy D., and Carol Hymowitz. "Hot Topics of the '90s." *The Wall Street Journal Centennial Edition,* June 23, 1989, p. A22.

19 The initial response of many U.S. companies: Chandler, Alfred D. "The Enduring Logic of Industrial Success." *Harvard Business Review,* March–April 1990, p. 130.

21 Fifteen years ago: Johnson, Robert. "With Its Spirit Shaken But Unbent, Cummins Shows Decade's Scars." *The Wall Street Journal,* December 13, 1989, p. A1.

CHAPTER 2

24 James Spackey, a publications manager: Spackey, James. "The RIPPing of Mid-Managers." *Newsweek,* April 18, 1988, p. 10.

25 The first time this happened: Personal interview.

25 After college, I worked: Personal contribution.

27 I hired about 30 managers: Personal interview.

28 The first time it happened to me: Personal interview.

29 Joan Learn, president of The Greenwich Group: Beaudoin, Tina. "Pushed Out of the Nest and Flying." *Management Review,* September 1988, p. 10.

29 When I was downsized: Personal interview.

30 About 20 percent of all managers: Beaudoin, Tina. "Pushed Out of the Nest and Flying."

30 My attitude toward working: Personal interview.

31 Employers may offer: "The End of Corporate Loyalty?" *Business Week,* August 4, 1986, p. 45.

31 In late 1989, it was reported: Carroll, Paul B. "IBM Expected to Unveil Plan to Cut Costs." *The Wall Street Journal,* December 5, 1989, p. A3.

32 Q. How did they handle: Personal interview.

33 One employee for a large office-equipment company: Jacobs, Deborah L. "The Growing Legal Battle Over Employee Waivers." *New York Times,* October 29, 1989.

34 And a 1989 survey: "Labor Letter." *The Wall Street Journal,* January 2, 1990.

Page

35 Jim White is a volunteer: *National Business Employment Weekly,* October 29, 1989, p. 14.
35 That's shown clearly by: Sandholtz, Kurt. "Executives in Transition." *National Business Employment Weekly,* August 27, 1989, p. 9.
36 This is also shown by the fact: Sandholtz. "Executives in Transition."

CHAPTER 3

41 They usually get a little bit: Personal interview.
42 After AT&T pared 25,000 employees: Kupfer, Andrew. "Bob Allen Rattles the Cages at AT&T," *Fortune,* June 19, 1989, p. 66.
43 When I read about the reactions: Personal interview.
43 I was a middle manager for a small division: Personal interview.
44 I never saw so much anxiety: Personal contribution.
44 It took me a long time: Personal interview.
45 My company has gone through: Seminar participant.
45 Unfortunately, says psychological consultant David M. Noer: Noer, David M. "Layoff Survivor Sickness." Presentation at the American Management Association Human Resources Conference, Nashville, Tennessee, April 27, 1989.
46 For example, take a company of 1,200 people: Personal interview.
46 Quite honestly, I feel overworked: Byrne, John A. "Caught in the Middle." *Business Week,* September 12, 1988, p. 80.
47 Salary's not everything: Personal interview.
48 As one human resources manager: Personal interview.
49 Average total CEO pay was $624,999: Byrne, John A. "For Whom Were the Golden Eighties Most Golden?" *Business Week,* May 7, 1990, p. 60.
49 For example, the Hay Group: *CompFlash,* January 1990.
49 For example, when First Interstate Bancorp's: McCoy, Charles. "First Interstate's Chief Will Soon Be Gone, But Not Its Problems." *The Wall Street Journal,* January 18, 1990, p. A1.
50 The CEO froze wages: Personal interview.

Page

50   While our salary increases: Drucker, Peter F. *The Frontiers of Management.* New York: Harper & Row, 1986, p. 139.

51   Executive compensation has become all reward: Verespej, Michael A. "Executives Win, Workers Lose." *Industry Week,* July 17, 1989.

51   As a case in point: The top three executives: Byrne, John A. "Pay Stubs of the Rich and Corporate." *Business Week,* May 7, 1990, p. 56.

51   These goodies include: Silk, Leonard. "Rich and Poor: The Gap Widens." *New York Times,* May 12, 1989, p. D2.

52   Another Wyatt Company survey: Kramon, Glenn. "Employers of 90's: Caught in Middle," *New York Times,* February 21, 1989, p. D2.

52   Corporations today are making: Freudenheim, Milt. "Limiting Outlays for Retirees," *New York Times,* September 12, 1989, p. D2.

53   As Peter Kelly, a Chicago lawyer: Schmitt, Richard B. "Retirees Fight Cuts in Health," *The Wall Street Journal,* December 8, 1988.

53   At our company, we looked forward: Personal interview.

54   A 1989 survey of 400 managers: "Labor Letter," *The Wall Street Journal,* January 16, 1990, p. A1.

54   A 1986 survey done for *Business Week:* Nussbaum, Bruce. "The End of Corporate Loyalty?" *Business Week,* August 4, 1986, p. 49.

54   A 1988 study of 1,200 middle managers: Byrne. "Caught in the Middle."

54   A 1989 survey of managers: "Labor Letter," *The Wall Street Journal,* June 6, 1989.

CHAPTER 4

57   It's tempting to say: Personal interview with John Clizbe, psychological consultant with Nordli, Wilson Associates.

58   A senior manager: Personal interview.

59   Often the first employees: Willis, Rod. "What's Happening to America's Middle Managers." *Management Review Special Reports* (undated).

Page

60 When we offered a good severance package: Seminar participant.

60 Hewlett-Packard, for example: Tomasko, Robert M. *Downsizing*. New York: AMACON, 1987, p. 155.

61 Exxon seemed to respond: Deutsch, Claudia H. "The Giant With a Black Eye." *New York Times,* April 2, 1989.

61 Another major oil spill: Sullivan, Allana. "Stretched Thin: Exxon's Restructuring in the Past Is Blamed for Recent Accidents." *The Wall Street Journal,* March 16, 1990, p. A1.

61 The threat of being acquired: Personal contribution.

62 That the distractions of restructurings: Ramirez, Anthony. "Avon Finds Source of Slide in Its Gift Sales: High Prices." *New York Times,* November 1, 1989.

62 In the case of leveraged buyouts: Murray, Thomas J. "For Downsizers, the Real Misery Is to Come." *Business Month,* February 1989, p. 72.

62 The rise in U.S. corporate outlays: Markoff, John. "A Corporate Lag in Research Funds Is Causing Worry." *New York Times,* January 23, 1990, p. A1.

63 In 1988 Duracell, Inc.: Clark, Lindley H., Jr. and Alfred L. Malabre, Jr., "Eroding R&D," *The Wall Street Journal,* November 16, 1988.

63 Prime Computer, Inc. is another example: Clark and Malabre, "Eroding R&D."

64 Business writer Max Holland: "Are LBOs Bad News for R&D?" *Challenges,* January 1989, p. 7.

64 It's pretty hard: Personal interview.

66 AT&T has paid: Murray. "For Downsizers, the Real Misery Is to Come," p. 71.

66 Employee stress is a function: Personal interview.

66 Because management can't guarantee: Personal interview.

67 A 1989 Towers Perrin survey found: *National Business Employment Weekly,* October 1, 1989, p. 29.

68 When a manager began tracking: Ansberry, Clare and Carol Hymowitz. "Kodak Chief Is Trying, For the Fourth Time, to Trim Firm's Costs," *The Wall Street Journal,* September 19, 1989, p. A-18.

68 A case in point is General Electric's: O'Boyle, Thomas F. "Chilling Tale: GE Refrigerator Woes." *The Wall Street Journal,* May 7, 1990, p. A1.

Page

69 Management did not go: Personal interview.
70 *The Chainsaw.* Climbing through: Horton, Thomas R. Speech before British Telecom Corporation, New York, October 28, 1988.
71 Downsizing was pretty much: Personal interview.
71 When the oil company announced: Murray. "For Downsizers, the Real Misery Is to Come," p. 72.
72 A classic example is: Willis, Rod. "What's Happening to America's Middle Managers?" *Management Review,* January 1987, p. 28.
73 Steve Snow, 36, went to work: Castro, Janice. "Where Did the Gung-Ho Go?" *Time,* September 11, 1989, p. 54.
73 Simple as the concept of offering: Lord, Virginia M. "Voluntary Programs: A Painless Way to Downsize." Career Center Bulletin 6, no. 2 (1988), p. 4.
74 Employee demoralization reached: Ansberry and Hymowitz. "Kodak Chief Is Trying, For the Fourth Time, to Trim Firm's Costs."
74 Quite a few people say: Personal interview.
75 The layoffs were done: Personal interview.
75 I think we did a good job: Personal interview.
75 Bunker Ramo was: Personal interview.
76 After the first downsizing: Personal interview.
76 In 1987 General Motors laid off: Murray. "For Downsizers, the Real Misery Is to Come."
77 The acquiring company: Personal interview.
78 The lead bank's people came in: Personal interview.
78 Employee dissatisfaction with: Security consultant Dennis Dalton, quoted in *The Wall Street Journal,* October 19, 1989.

CHAPTER 5

81 At the Sixth General Assembly: Pascarella, Perry. "Visionary Leadership Will Design the Future," *Industry Week,* August 21, 1989, p. 48.
82 The biggest pitfall for a corporate leader: Byrd, Richard E. "Corporate Leadership Skills: A New Synthesis." *Organizational Dynamics Special Reports,* 1988.

Page

83 Values are meaningful only if: Leavitt, Harold. *Corporate Pathfinders,* Homewood, Ill: Dow Jones-Irwin, 1986.

85 In 1965 individual shareholders represented: Bartlett, Sarah. "Big Funds Pressing for Voice in Management of Companies." *New York Times,* Febraury 23, 1990.

86 By the end of 1989, institutions owned: Melloan, George. "Champion's CEO Ponders the Corporate 'Ownership' Riddle." *The Wall Street Journal,* June 6, 1989.

86 Andrew C. Sigler, chairman and CEO: Melloan. "Champion's CEO Ponders the Corporate 'Ownership' Riddle."

86 The investors' role is so small: Bartlett, Sarah. "New Type of Owner Emerges in Wave of Company Buyouts." *New York Times,* November 8, 1988.

87 The raiders are surely right to assert: Drucker, Peter. "Peter Drucker's 1990s," *The Economist,* October 21, 1989, p. 23.

87 One disillusioned 20-year worker: Nussbaum, Bruce. "The End of Corporate Loyalty?" *Business Week,* August 4, 1986, p. 42.

87 A U.S. public company is controlled: Boudette, Neal E. "Is Short Term Really the American Way?" *Industry Week,* June 5, 1989, p. 12.

88 Champion's Andrew C. Sigler puts it: Melloan. "Champion's CEO Ponders the Corporate 'Ownership' Riddle."

88 A similar example involves: Kassebaum, Nancy L. "How About Taxing Pension Fund Profits?" *New York Times,* August 30, 1989.

88 The shareholders extract the maximum: Personal interview.

89 NCR Chairman and CEO Charles E. Exley, Jr: Boudette. "Is Short Term Really the American Way?"

89 Robert D. Ferris, executive vice president: Ferris, Robert D. "Reining in Restructuring Mania." *Directors & Boards,* Spring 1989.

91 Management has been described: Horton, Thomas R. *What Works for Me.* New York: Random House, 1986, p. 2.

92 But in a study of 214 large U.S. companies: Crystal Graef S. "At the Top: An Explosion of Pay Packages." *New York Times Magazine,* December 3, 1989, p. 25.

92 And a study of the relationship: Fierman, Jaclyn. "The People Who Set the CEO's Pay." *Fortune,* March 12, 1990, p. 58.

Page

92   A study by polling firm: Farnham, Alan. "The Trust Gap." *Fortune,* December 4, 1989, p. 56.

92   I recently made presentations: Personal interview.

93   We CEOs spend a lot of time: Personal interview.

93   Psychological consultant John Clizbe: Personal interview.

93   These companies are dysfunctional: Farnham. "The Trust Gap."

94   We held five separate meetings among our: Personal interview.

94   Another example of the non-isolationist leader: Deutsch, Claudia H. "Colgate's Next Trick: Controlling the Chaos." *New York Times,* August 6, 1989.

96   Henry B. Schacht, CEO of Cummins Engine Company: Bartlett, Sarah. "Books on Greed Worry Wall St." *New York Times,* February 12, 1990.

96   In November that year: "Guilty Plea by Ex-Officer of Beech-Nut," *New York Times,* November 14, 1989.

97   On February 27, 1990, Northrop Corporation: Stevenson, Richard W. "Northrop Guilty Plea Submitted." *New York Times,* February 28, 1990.

97   As part of the plea bargain: Wartzman, Rick. "Northrop's Settlement of U.S. Fraud Case Also Ends Separate Inquiry into MX, B-2," *The Wall Street Journal,* March 1, 1990.

97   Small wonder that a 1989 Louis Harris poll: "The Public Is Willing to Take Business On." *Business Week,* May 29, 1989, p. 29.

97   Another Harris poll in the same year: Modic, Stanley J. "Whatever It Is, It's Not Working." *Industry Week,* July 17, 1989, p. 27.

97   ITT managers quickly learned: Deutsch, Claudia H. "Reforging the 'Geneen Machine.'" *New York Times,* May 21, 1989.

98   Marvin Bower once observed that: Bower, Marvin. *The Will to Manage.* New York: McGraw-Hill, 1966, p. 25.

98   A 1989 survey by two Columbia Unversity: "Doing the 'Right' Thing Has Its Repercussions." *Wall Street Journal,* January 25, 1990.

98   Underlying the skills and capabilities: Horton, Thomas R. *What Works for Me,* p. 398.

CHAPTER 6

Page

103 In fact, it may even be beneficial: *Boardroom Reports,* November 1, 1989, p. 2, quoting George Bailey, principal, Cresap, a unit of Towers Perrin, San Francisco.

103 During the 1980s, Du Pont: Personal interview.

105 The resource head's office: Personal interview.

105 Another admirable example of: Personal interview.

106 Strategic planning requires: Marks, Lee, and Philip Harold Mirvis. "The Merger Syndrome." *Psychology Today,* October 1986, p. 27.

106 It shouldn't be a: Personal interview.

107 I looked around the room: Personal interview.

107 Too many companies: McCann, Nancy Dodd. "Will Your Acquisition Be an Asset or an Albatross?" presentation at the American Management Association Human Resources Conference, April 26, 1989, Nashville, Tennessee.

109 Norbert J. Kubilus, vice president: Personal interview.

109 Research shows that the more: Marks and Mirvis. "The Merger Syndrome."

110 In an *Industry Week* article: Purser, John R. Purser + Associates, "Straight Talk at Merger Time." *Industry Week,* June 20, 1988, p. 78.

110 When times are bad: Personal interview.

111 Merck & Company, which in 1990: "Labor Letter." *The Wall Street Journal,* October 10, 1989, p. A-10.

112 IBM is one of them: Solomon, Jolie. "A Fine Line." *The Wall Street Journal,* December 8, 1989, p. R16.

113 To be successful, early-retirement packages: Hoffman, Jeffrey S. "Sweetening Early-Retirement Programs." *Personnel,* March 1990, p. 18.

113 Perhaps the most generous package: Bhatia, Gauri. "Severance Pay: Less Pain, Some Gain." *CFO Magazine,* April 1989, p. 61.

113 Dubbed a "tin parachute" by those: Bhatia. "Severance Pay: Less Pain, Some Gain."

114 Eastman Kodak announced a similar program: Hymowitz, Carol. "Kodak Gives 'Parachutes' to Workers." *The Wall Street Journal,* January 2, 1990, p. B-1.

Page

115 A good example is Mobil's: Personal interview.

115 A full-service outplacement firm should: "Outplacement and Career Management Services the Right Way." Brochure, Right Associates, Philadelphia, 1989.

116 Texas Instruments, Inc.'s operation: Sheridan, John H. "Lean But Not Mean." *Industry Week,* February 19, 1990, p. 53.

117 When we had to cut 30 percent: Personal interview.

118 As Robert Tomasko notes: Tomasko, Robert. *Downsizing.* New York: AMACOM, 1987.

118 There's an understandable temptation: Personal interview with John Clizbe, psychological consultant, Nordli, Wilson Associates.

118 After the frightening San Francisco earthquake: Navarro, Mireya. "Message to a City's Rattled Populace: Try to Talk About It." *New York Times,* October 20, 1989.

118 This allows employees: Willis, Rod. "What's Happening to America's Middle Managers?" *Management Review,* January 1987, p. 28.

119 First, the company must revisit: Personal interview.

120 During restructurings such as mergers: Personal interview.

CHAPTER 7

122 The only real replacement for today's manager: Yoder, Dale. "The Changing Role of Management—Innovation Is In." *Stanford Graduate School of Business Bulletin* 36, No. 1.

123 ... which one GM manager described as: Byrne, John A. "Middle Managers—Are They An Endangered Species?" *Business Week,* September 12, 1988, p. 80.

126 Management tells us they want: Johnson, Leonard W., and Alan L. Frohman, "Identifying and Closing the Gap in the Middle of Organizations." *The Academy of Management Executives,* May 1989, p. 107.

126 In a 1989 survey of 101 human resources executives: Mercer, Michael W. "The HR Department as a Profit Center." *Personnel,* April 1989, p. 34.

127 Consultant Franck A. de Chambeau points out: De Chambeau, Franck A. "Strategically Managing Human Resources."

Page

Presentation at American Management Association Human Resources Conference, Nashville, Tennessee, April 27, 1989.

128 The first step is to identify deficiencies: Personal interview.

128 Among the steps recommended: Coruzzi, Celeste A. "The Work of Organization Development: Benefits for Large System Change." Presentation at American Management Association Human Resources Conference, Nashville, Tennessee, April 27, 1989.

129 We recognized that some people have: Personal interview.

131 Managers need to be more global: Personal interview.

131 Our middle managers are very competent functionally: Personal interview.

132 Managers must learn to: Finkelman, Daniel P. "If the Customer Has an Itch, Scratch It." *New York Times,* May 14, 1989.

132 "Managers have to see their roles as: Tichy, Noel, and Ram Charan, "Speed, Simplicity, Self-Confidence: An Interview with Jack Welch." *Harvard Business Review,* September-October 1989, p. 112.

132 They resent losing control over: Schlesinger, Leonard A., and Barry Oshry, "Quality of Work Life and the Manager: Muddle in the Middle." *Organization Dynamics Special Reports,* 1988, p. 63.

133 Many managers believe that there is: Conner, Daryl R. "Chords of Change." Round-table discussion, *World,* Summer 1988, p. 36.

133 Management professor and author: Kanter, Rosabeth Moss. "The New Managerial Work." *Harvard Business Review,* November–December 1989, p. 85.

133 In 1985 there was one computer: Dreyfuss, Joel. "Catching the Computer Wave." *Fortune,* September 26, 1988, p. 78.

133 Interestingly enough, a study of productivity: Gellerman, Saul W. "Turn Production Goals Into Employee Goals." *Supervisory Management,* November 1963.

134 Many managers will find it difficult: Personal interview.

135 Some of our managers felt: Personal interview.

136 In one sense, maintains management writer: Kuriloff, Arthur H. "Another Look at Leadership Potential." *Management Review,* February 1968.

137 One example of this is provided: Reid, Peter C. *Well-Made in America.* New York: McGraw-Hill, 1989.

Page

138 This is a program we are driving down: Personal interview.
138 Xerox is another company that: Deets, Norman, and Dr. Richard Morano, "Xerox's Strategy for Changing Management Styles." *Management Review Special Reports* (undated).
142 At Mobil, we are redefining: Personal interview.
142 Many managers are too much into: Personal interview.
143 Remember the theory that: Tichy and Charan. "Speed, Simplicity, Self-Confidence."
143 Span of control will be broadened: Personal interview.
143 One way to attack the problem: "Downsizing Mistake." *Boardroom Reports,* October 15, 1989, p. 2.
146 Back in the mid-1970s: Mandell, Barbara, and Susan Kohler-Gray. "Management Development That Values Diversity." *Personnel,* March 1990, p. 41.
146 Aetna Life & Casualty in Hartford, Connecticut: Bennett, Amanda. "As Pool of Skilled Help Tightens, Firms Move to Broaden Their Role." *The Wall Street Journal,* May 8, 1989, p. A1.
147 We had downsized our sales and marketing: Personal interview.
147 Historically, we had very strict: Personal interview.
148 Technology created the early organization form: Norton, David P. "Chords of Change." Round-table discussion, *World,* Summer 1988, p. 36.
149 In the course of the 5½-day session: Kiechel, Walter III. "The Organization that Learns." *Fortune,* March 12, 1990, p. 132.
150 In the future, says Hudson Institute's: Main, Jeremy. "The Winning Organization." *Fortune,* September 26, 1988, p. 50.
150 Psychologist Harrison G. Gough defines: Raudsepp, Eugene. "How Flexible Is Your Operating Style?" *National Business Employment Weekly,* September 3, 1989, p. 12.
151 We are moving toward a fluid system: Toffler, Alvin. "Chords of Change." Round-table discussion, *World,* Summer 1988, p. 36.

CHAPTER 8

153 David L. Birch, president of: College Placement Council news release, January 1990.

Page

153 For years, employers treated: Pare, Terence P. "The Uncommitted Class of 1989." *Fortune,* June 5, 1989, p. 199.

153 Dr. Birch believes that: College Placement Council news release, January 1990.

155 Organizational psychologist Kate Ludeman writes: Ludeman, Kate. "Bosses, Embrace Your Workers!" *New York Times,* May 14, 1989, Sec. 1, p. 2.

160 We've grown up in a culture: Kilborn, Peter T. "Companies that Temper Ambition." *New York Times,* February 27, 1990, p. D1.

160 PG&E tackles this perception problem: Kilborn. "Companies that Temper Ambition."

161 Eastman Kodak's career development plan: Cahill, Cindy M. "Career Development: Eastman Kodak's Approach." Presentation at American Management Association Human Resources Conference, Nashville, Tennessee, April 28, 1989.

161 The manager who wants to be: Personal interview.

161 For example, a survey of 325: Fritz, Norma R. "Middle Managers' High Hopes." *Personnel,* July 1989, p. 4.

162 A 1988 survey by Wick and Company: Wick, Calhoun W., and Carl R. Weinberg. "Are Today's Career Development Strategies Creating a Generation of Disappointment?" *Career Center Bulletin* 6, Columbia Unversity's No. 2, 1988.

163 When our company agreed to write: Wick and Weinberg. "Today's Career Development Strategies."

164 Robert H. Schaffer, author of: Schaffer, Robert H. "How to Tap the 'Zest Factor.'" *New York Times,* May 7, 1989.

164 A striking example is provided by: Kleinfield, N. R. "How 'Strykeforce' Beat the Clock." *New York Times,* March 25, 1990.

165 When a company well known for its: Horton, Thomas R. "Why Can't We Get It Right?" *Management Review,* April 1990, p. 4.

167 Like a lot of good ideas: Personal interview.

169 In an *Industry Week* readership survey: Verespej, Michael A. "Merit Raises 'A Joke.'" *Industry Week,* February 19, 1990, p. 73.

169 According to a Hay Group study: Lee, Tony. "Performance Pays Off When Salary Hikes Are Set." *National Business Employment Weekly,* October 19, 1989, p. 31.

Page

169 In order not to get the raise: Waldman, Steven, and Betsy Roberts. "Grading 'Merit Pay.'" *Newsweek,* November 14, 1988, p. 46.

170 Look at the results of a: Weiss, Stuart. "The Sad Saga of Variable Pay." *Business Month,* April 1990, p. 74.

170 A 1989 survey by Hewitt Associates: *Compflash,* May 1989, p. 1.

171 Marc J. Wallace, Jr., business professor at: Weiss. "The Sad Saga of Variable Pay."

171 A 1990 *Industry Week* survey: Verespej. "Merit Raises: 'A Joke.'"

172 A group of eight middle managers: Bennett, Amanda. "Caught in the Middle." *The Wall Street Journal,* April 18, 1990.

173 "Companies want to get away: Verespej, Michael A. "Executives Win, Workers Lose." *Industry Week,* July 17, 1989.

174 An example is the system used by: Personal interview.

174 "Last year I got the biggest bonus: Byrne, John A. "Middle Managers: Are They an Endangered Species?" *Business Week,* September 12, 1988.

175 One way to ameliorate this problem: Lawler, Edward E. III, and Gerald E. Ledford, Jr., "Skill-Based Pay: A Concept That's Catching On." *Management Review Special Reports,* 1987, p. 26.

176 Our new appraisal form incorporates: Personal interview.

CHAPTER 9

179 I think it is a matter of bringing: Personal interview.

179 Hay Group's Peter Gelfond sees: Personal interview.

180 One consultant reports that: Farnham, Alan. "The Trust Gap." *Fortune,* December 4, 1989, p. 56.

180 Tom Nies, CEO and president of: Modic, Stanley J. "Cincom Bets Big on People Power." *Industry Week,* August 21, 1989, p. 23.

181 Good internal communications is a top: Personal contribution.

181 Studies by the Hay Group show: Farnham. "The Trust Gap."

Page

182 Burson-Marsteller, a large and successful: Horton, Thomas R. *What Works for Me.* New York: Random House, 1986.

182 For example, when Carnegie Mellon University: Field, Anne R. "O Ye of Little Faith." *Business Month,* April 1990, p. 7.

183 Employees want to know how they: Personal interview.

185 Two of these are Ken Iverson and Herb Kelleher: Farnham. "The Trust Gap."

186 We were basically honest with: Personal interview.

186 *Fortune* reports that a: O'Reilly, Brian. "Is Your Company Asking Too Much?" *Fortune,* March 12, 1990, p. 38.

187 According to the New York Business Group: Cohen, Julie A. "High Anxiety Can Lower Profits." *Management Review,* January 1990, p. 7.

188 Julie A. Cohen, in *Management Review*: Cohen. "High Anxiety Can Lower Profits."

189 For example, AT&T has: Fowler, Elizabeth M. "More Stress Found in the Workplace." *New York Times,* September 12, 1989.

189 And Apple Computer offers: O'Reilly. "Is Your Company Asking Too Much?"

189 In 1989, according to the *Japan Times:* Sabotta, Steven. Letter to *New York Times,* March 19, 1990.

190 Listen to Robert Paulson, director of: O'Reilly, "Is Your Company Asking Too Much?" p. 37.

191 A survey of 1,000 employees: "Goodbye 60-Hour Weeks." *National Business Employment Weekly,* July 16, 1989, p. 31.

191 As Betty Holcomb, senior editor of: Holcomb, Betty. Letter to *Harvard Business Review.* January–February 1990, p. 195.

191 Seventy percent of women with children: Rodgers, Fran Sussner, and Charles Rodgers, "Business and the Facts of Family Life." *Harvard Business Review,* November–December 1989, p. 121.

192 Says Faith Wohl, director of: Lewin, Tamar. " 'Mommy Career Track' Sets Off a Furor." *New York Times,* March 8, 1989, p. A18.

192 And *Working Mother's* Betty Holcomb: Holcomb. Letter to *Harvard Business Review.*

194 Michael Maccoby, president of: Maccoby, Michael. Letter to *New York Times,* May 21, 1989.

Page

194 IBM, Johnson & Johnson, NCNB: Rodgers and Rodgers. "Business and the Facts of Family Life."

195 We don't expect a lifetime commitment: Biodolillo, Deborah. Letter to *New York Times*, May 21, 1989.

196 In our advice to managers: Personal interview.

199 Part of the new contract is that: Personal interview.

201 Employees are expected to assume: Cahill, Cindy M. "Career Development: Eastman Kodak's Approach." Presentation at American Management Association's Human Resources Conference, Nashville, Tennessee, April 28, 1989.

204 To avoid these harmful effects of stress: Huddle, Donald P. "Stress on the Job? Here's What to Do About It." *Supervisory Management,* July 1967.

CHAPTER 10

205 Businesses will undergo more: Drucker, Peter. "Peter Drucker's 1990s." *The Economist,* October 21, 1989, p. 23.

207 As GE's Jack Welch has said: "Managing Now for the 1990s." *Fortune,* September 26, 1988, p. 44.

208 In April 1990 *The Wall Street Journal:* Solomon, Jolie, and Gilbert Fuchsberg. "Fresh Wave of Cutbacks Is Hitting All Sectors, Leaving Few Options." *The Wall Street Journal,* April 9, 1990.

209 *Business Week* wondered if: Byrne, John A. "Middle Managers: Are They An Endangered Species?" *Business Week,* September 12, 1988.

210 GE's Jack Welch put it well: Tichy, Noel, and Ram Charan, "Speed, Simplicity, Self-Confidence: An Interview with Jack Welch." *Harvard Business Review,* September–October 1989, p. 112.

210 For example, Walter Kiechel III suggests: Kiechel, Walter III. "The Organization that Learns." *Fortune,* March 12, 1990, p. 132.

211 In 1968 Robert M. Hutchins proposed: Hutchins, Robert M. *The Learning Society.* New York: Frederick A. Praeger, 1968.

212 A two-year probe by the: Day, Charles R. Jr. "You're Flunking, Too!" *Industry Week,* June 5, 1989, p. 50.

Page

212 Among middle managers who recognize: Welter, Therese R. "IW Readers Play Futurist." *Industry Week,* June 20, 1988, p. 71.

212 Early in 1990, *The Wall Street Journal:* Karr, Albert R. "Labor Letter," *The Wall Street Journal,* January 23, 1990, p. A1.

215 In early 1990, a *Fortune* article: Dumaine, Brian. "Who Needs a Boss?" *Fortune,* May 7, 1990.

216 On top is a steering team: Dumaine. "Who Needs a Boss?"

216 A book-acquisition editor: Conversation with Adrienne Hickey, February 13, 1990.

218 In the spring of 1990: Byrne, John A. "Pay Stubs of the Rich and Corporate." *Business Week,* May 7, 1990, p. 56.

218 Roger B. Smith, retiring chairman: Levin, Doron P. "G.M. Seeks Sharp Increases in Top Executives' Pensions." *New York Times,* May 3, 1990, p. D1.

220 The horse latitudes was an area: Ferrigno, Robert. *The Horse Latitudes.* New York: William Morrow & Company, 1990.

SUGGESTED READINGS

This is a partial list of materials we have found to be useful and interesting. Listed by author in alphabetical order.

Bell, Robert. *Surviving the 10 Ordeals of the Takeover.* New York: AMACOM, 1988.

Bennett, Amanda. *The Death of the Organization Man.* New York: William Morrow & Company, 1990.

Bower, Marvin. *The Will to Manage.* New York: McGraw-Hill, 1966.

Bridges, William. *Surviving Corporate Transition.* New York: Doubleday, 1988.

Byrne, John A. "Caught in the Middle." *Business Week,* September 12, 1988, p. 80.

Drucker, Peter F. *The Frontiers of Management: Where Tomorrow's Decisions Are Being Shaped Today.* New York: Harper & Row, 1986.

Farnham, Alan. "The Trust Gap." *Fortune,* December 4, 1989, p. 56.

Galbraith, John Kenneth. *The New Industrial State.* Boston: Houghton Mifflin, 1967.

Jenks, James, and Brian Zevnik. *Managers Caught in the Crunch: Turning a Job Crisis into a Career Opportunity.* New York: Franklin Watts, 1988.

Kanter, Donald L., and Phillip H. Mirvis. *The Cynical Americans: Living and Working in an Age of Discontent and Disillusion.* San Francisco: Jossey-Bass, 1989.

Kanter, Rosabeth Moss. *The Change Masters.* New York: Simon & Schuster, 1983.

Kanter, Rosabeth Moss. *When Giants Learn to Dance: Mastering the Challenges of Strategy, Management, and Careers in the 1990s.* New York: Simon & Schuster, 1989.

Mills, D. Quinn. *The IBM Lesson: The Profitable Art of Full Employment.* New York: Times Books, 1988.

Morgan, Gareth. *Riding Waves of Change.* San Francisco: Jossey-Bass, 1988.

Morin, William J., and James C. Cabrera. *Parting Company: How to Survive the Loss of a Job and Find Another Successfully*. New York: Harcourt Brace Jovanovich, 1982.

Morin, William J., and Lyle Yorks. *Dismissal: There Is No Easy Way but There Is a Better Way*. New York: Drake Beam Morin, 1990.

Nussbaum, Bruce. "The End of Corporate Loyalty?" *Business Week*, August 4, 1986, p. 49.

Tomasko, Robert M. *Downsizing: Reshaping the Corporation for the Future*. Revised edition. New York: AMACOM, 1990.

Tuller, Lawrence W. *The Battle-Weary Executive*. Homewood, Ill.: Dow Jones-Irwin, 1990.

Walton, Clarence C. *The Moral Manager*. New York: Ballinger, 1988.

Index